The Future of a Negation

The Future of a Negation

Reflections on the Question
of Genocide

Alain Finkielkraut
L'avenir d'une négation: Réflexion
sur la question du génocide
Translated by Mary Byrd Kelly
with an Introduction by
Richard J. Golsan

University of Nebraska Press
Lincoln & London

Publication of this translation
was assisted by a grant from the French Ministry of
Culture. © Éditions du Seuil, 1982. Translation
introduction © 1998 by the University of Nebraska
Press. All rights reserved Manufactured in the
United States of America

Library of Congress Cataloging-in-Publication Data

Finkielkraut, Alain.
[Avenir d'une négation. English]
The future of a negation: reflections on the question
of genocide / Alain Finkielkraut; translated by
Mary Byrd Kelly; with an introduction by Richard
J. Golsan.   p. cm. – (Texts and contexts)
Includes bibliographical references and index.
ISBN 0-8032-2000-6 (cloth : alkaline paper)
1. Holocaust denial. 2. Socialism and antisemitism.
I. Title. II. Series.
D804.355.F5613 1998 179.7–dc21
97-30297 CIP

To my parents

Contents

Translator's Note

Throughout *The Future of a Negation* I have, wherever possible, used the original English for Finkielkraut's citations of works written in English. Similarly I have, wherever possible, used published English translations of French works that Finkielkraut cites or of works in other foreign languages that Finkielkraut cites in their French translation. Otherwise, translations of passages cited are my own renderings of the French version.

At the end of the book, two additional sorts of notes are interspersed among Finkielkraut's original footnotes. The first are those of Richard J. Golsan, who wrote the book's introduction; they are intended to clarify the historical context surrounding aspects of the book with which the American reader may not be familiar. The second sort are those I added in order to explain a word or phrase that has no real equivalent in English or that has a specific cultural connotation in French. Both Professor Golsan's notes and mine carry the appropriate attribution to distinguish them from the author's.

M.B.K.

Introduction

Negationism in France: The Past and Present of an Illusion

In late June 1996, publicity posters appeared in bookshop windows and newsstand displays throughout France announcing the upcoming issue of the popular French weekly magazine *L'Evénement du jeudi*. Frequently used by *L'EDJ* and other French magazines to attract readership, these posters regularly announce provocative cover stories and include striking photographs. The poster for the 27 June–3 July issue was no exception. In bold red, black, and white letters, the poster announced "The Holocaust: The Victory of the Revisionists." The headline was superimposed on a crisp color photograph of the familiar bearded face of an aging priest known throughout France as "Father Pierre." When the issue of *L'EDJ* appeared on the newsstands, it sold out within hours.

While the headline alone was certainly shocking enough to attract a large readership, it was the juxtaposition of the announcement of the victory of the "revisionists" with the photo of Father Pierre that brought into sharp focus the latest episode of what has come to be known in France as *le négationnisme*— "negationism," or the denial of the Holocaust.[1] Shocking as it may have been in 1996, such "negationism" had already been identified and brilliantly dissected in 1982 by the young public intellectual Alain Finkielkraut in *The Future of a Negation*.

xi

Introduction

The continuing relevance of Finkielkraut's critique was vividly apparent in November 1995, when Pierre Guillaume, director of the ultraleftist La Vieille Taupe ("the Old Mole") publishing house and a veteran "negationist" himself, announced the forthcoming publication of a new book by Roger Garaudy entitled *Les Mythes fondateurs de la politique israélienne* (The founding myths of Israeli politics).[2] Despite its grandiose title, the book is on close inspection little more than a rehash of earlier "scientific proofs" that the Nazi plan to exterminate the Jews was a myth; that the gas chambers, where they had actually functioned, were used for delousing; and that the Allies were at least as intent on exterminating the Germans as the Germans were of ridding themselves of the Jews. Like many of its predecessors, Garaudy's book also denounces the Nuremberg trials as "show trials" where the "victors' justice" unjustly blamed the war on the vanquished while covering over the Allies' responsibilities. As Garaudy bitterly remarks, "Neither Churchill, nor Stalin, nor Truman was ever in the dock for war crimes" (100). The only relatively new twists to Garaudy's "negationism" are the extent, nature, and vehemence of his attacks on Israeli and Euro-American racism.[3] Comparing Menachem Begin's racism to Hitler's and insisting that there is no real difference between the two (24), Garaudy goes on to argue that the "myth" of the Holocaust is essential to Israel in order to justify its own form of aggression—"Zionist colonialism"—and its oppression of the Palestinians. Israeli power, in turn, serves the global ambitions of the United States, which itself seeks to subjugate the Third World and to appropriate and control the flow of all Middle Eastern oil (8).

Broadening his attacks on Euro-American racism, Garaudy also asserts that what Hitler did to "whites" was no different than what European and American colonialists did to people of color for centuries. He argues, in fact, that the

Introduction

American "genocide" of black Africans during the period of slave trading dwarfs Hitler's supposed genocide of the Jews. Using a "scientific" logic and statistical "evidence" that would make his fellow negationists proud, Garaudy argues that since ten to twenty million Africans were "deported" into slavery, and that for each deportee ten were killed in their efforts to elude capture and deportation, the real figure for the American "genocide" of black Africans is one hundred to two hundred million dead.[4]

Guillaume's announcement of the forthcoming publication of *Les Mythes fondateurs de la politique israélienne* was not simply intended to inform fellow "negationists" of a new book to their taste or to attract a few new converts. His strategy, according to Pierre-André Taguieff, was more complex.[5] First, Guillaume counted on some members of the press to publicize Garaudy's book by denouncing it. This, in turn, would inevitably result in lawsuits against Garaudy because in France, since the passage in May 1990 of the Gayssot Law, it is illegal to "contest the existence of one or more crimes against humanity as they are defined by Article Six of the Statute of the International Military Tribunal annexed to the London Accords of 8 August 1945." Named after a Communist deputy involved in drafting the legislation, the Gayssot Law has been roundly criticized by historians, intellectuals, and government officials who, like Simone Veil, believe that "one cannot impose a historical truth by law."[6] Being charged under such an unpopular and misguided law, the negationists—in this instance, Garaudy—could cast themselves in a more favorable light, even to the extent of assuming the role of victim in a legal controversy they themselves had set in motion.

The strategy worked to perfection, and at a press conference held on 18 April 1996 to discuss Garaudy's book and the legal controversy surrounding it, the author of *Les Mythes fondateurs de la politique israélienne* dropped another bomb. He removed from his hat a lengthy letter of support from his old friend, Father Pierre.

In order to understand Father Pierre's role in the controversy and the impact of his involvement, it is necessary to know something of the backgrounds of both Father Pierre and Roger Garaudy and the history of their relationship. Of the two men, Garaudy is the less interesting and certainly the less significant. In many ways a perfect example of Eric Fromm's "true believer," Garaudy has gone from one commitment or faith to another. At one time a militant Stalinist who denied the existence of the Gulag,[7] Garaudy became disaffected with communism, converted to Christianity, and then converted again, this time to Islam. As part of this most recent conversion, Garaudy became a passionate advocate of the Palestinian cause—hence his hatred of Israel and his challenge to its "founding myth," the Holocaust. A prolific writer whose works were once published by the likes of Gallimard and Presses Universitaires de France, Garaudy through his supporters has laid claim to a certain intellectual legitimacy in order to lend support to his recent revisionist claims. It is thus Roger Garaudy, the respected "philosopher," who has presented the latest evidence of the Holocaust "hoax" to the French public.

A loyal friend to Garaudy through all his metamorphoses, Father Pierre is an altogether different sort of figure, in terms both of his past and of his stature in contemporary France. Raised in a devoutly religious household in Lyons, the young Henry Groués (to use his real name) accompanied his father each Sunday to minister to the poor in hospices around the city.[8] On his own initiative he also frequented orphanages where, legend has it, he gave away his favorite toys. Sensing within himself a deeply religious vocation, Groués joined the Capuchin order, but medical problems forced him to give up monastery life and join the priesthood. A vicar in Grenoble when the Second World War broke out, Groués quickly joined the Resistance, taking as his nom de guerre "Father Pierre." During the war, Groués protected Jews, fought in the Vercors region, and at one point saved the life of Charles de Gaulle's younger brother. A true wartime hero, Groués received the War Cross and the Cross of the Resistance for his efforts.

In the postwar years, having permanently adopted his nom de guerre, Father Pierre entered politics. Joining the MRP (Mouvement Républicain Populaire),[9] he was elected deputy to the National Assembly. It was there that he met and befriended Roger Garaudy, who was serving as a Communist deputy at the time. Abandoning the MRP, Father Pierre joined the independent left and was defeated in the 1951 elections. A longtime defender of the poor and homeless, Father Pierre founded Emmaüs (an international organization to help the homeless help themselves) in 1949 and continued to militate on behalf of the downtrodden in a variety of circumstances for the next five decades. Public opinion polls indicated he was France's national conscience and the most popular Frenchman alive.

For years before his scandalous support of Garaudy and his negationist theses, however, Father Pierre had shown signs of poor judgment and prejudice bordering on racism. Having allowed into his inner circle of confidants and advisors individuals formerly involved with the Italian Red Brigades and closely linked to the Palestinian cause (one of these, Françoise Salvoni, informed Father Pierre that Garaudy's book was "not anti-Semitic"—a view Pierre accepted, since he had not read the book), Father Pierre on occasion spoke out on behalf of a former Red Brigader arrested in Italy for gun trafficking with Palestinians and criticized French police for investigating a language school in Paris supposedly harboring former Red Brigade members. In a different context, during the war in Bosnia, Father Pierre also denounced the massacre of Bosnians "even if they are Muslims." He later retracted this statement.

But Father Pierre's most troubling assertions, at least in light of his subsequent support of Garaudy, were those he made in the early 1990s concerning the Bible and specifically concerning the Book of Joshua.[10] To the shock and amazement of his interlocutors at the time, Father Pierre argued that the first crime against humanity, the first "Shoah," had been committed by the Jews themselves in their "genocide" of the Canaanites. In his view, this crime would compromise the Jews' claim to the Promised Land. Moreover, Father Pierre argued in another context that the "Zionist" excesses of today's Israelis made of them not victims but "executioners" in their own right. Assertions such as these, along with a call for a new debate on the existence of the Holocaust, were included in Father Pierre's letter of support to Garaudy distributed at the latter's press conference.

Called upon by outraged supporters and enemies alike to renounce his support of Garaudy, Father Pierre, already known for his stubbornness, not only held firm but upped the stakes of his commitment. In an interview in *Libération*, he ignored demands that he distance himself from Garaudy's negationist views and reiterated his call for a new debate on the historical reality of the Holocaust. In comments quoted in the National Front daily *Présent* on 21 June 1996, Father Pierre denounced what he called "a world-wide Zionist plot" and claimed that Zionists had adopted "attitudes identical to Hitler's on the issue of racism" and used the same murderous means in achieving their ends.[11]

Under pressure from LICRA (Ligue internationale contre le racisme et l'antisémitisme) Father Pierre finally backed away from his support of Garaudy, but the damage had already been done.[12] In lending his prestige even if only briefly to Garaudy, France's "saintliest man" had given a new legitimacy to negationism in the public view. In late spring and early summer 1996, signs asking "And what if Father Pierre were right?" appeared on the sides of overpasses crossing the beltway around Paris. Despite shock and disappointment in many quarters, polls indicated that Father Pierre's popularity had not diminished significantly, and among his fervent admirers, new doubts about the Holocaust were raised.[13] For why would a man who had devoted his life to fighting against human suffering lie about Auschwitz? In recruiting the individual who had for many come to personify postwar French humanitarianism, the negationists had in effect succeeded in finding the perfect weapon in their struggle to efface the most inhuman of crimes. For the leftist activist Gilles Perrault, Father Pierre was nothing less than the "Philippe Pétain of the 1990s." Like Pétain in 1940, he brought his enormous prestige to an evil cause and, through the sheer weight of his own celebrity, made that cause plausible to significant portions of the French public.[14]

As a number of commentators have noted, the implications of Father Pierre's support for his friend Roger Garaudy and his book in the spring of 1996 extend well beyond questions concerning the historical reality of the Holocaust and the existence of the gas chambers. The aims and ambitions of negationism as well as the ideological motives driving it are, especially in France, much more complex and indeed dangerous than the stated desires of the negationists to "set the record straight" would allow. Negationism constitutes, first of all, an expression of and an effort to "banalize" or legitimize anti-Semitism and, through attacks on "Zionism," to reintroduce it as a "threat" to be debated in the public forum.[15] In denouncing "Zionist"—read *Israeli*—racism, and comparing it in theory and practice to Hitlerian racism,

Introduction

Father Pierre not only contributed to what Taguieff labels a "conspirationalist judeophobia" but also through his person linked a traditional French Catholic anti-Semitism to a more current hatred of Israel.[16] The results, according to historians and philosophers including Pierre Vidal-Naquet and Bernard-Henri Lévy, were devastating. The negationists, in Vidal-Naquet's words, "had won." They were "in the process of inventing the anti-Semitism of the twenty-first century."[17] And while Father Pierre could certainly not be accused of recognizing or promoting negationism's most sinister design, that design remains, according to Robert Redeker, the continuation of the Holocaust in the present through its erasure in the past.[18]

Negationism is, of course, also intent on rewriting history and, as the example of Garaudy's book suggests, not just the details of the Holocaust itself. Garaudy's distortions embrace German and Allied motives during World War II, the Nuremberg trials, the American "genocide" of black Africans, and so on. Father Pierre's historical revisionism is perhaps even more egregious, since as Alain Finkielkraut notes, it conflates contemporary Israeli politics with the biblical massacres of the Canaanites.[19] Moreover, it implicitly compares the latter with the Nazi genocide of the Jews by describing the destruction of the Canaanites as the first "Shoah." The dangers of such comparisons are all too evident since, as the Historian's Debate in Germany revealed, they serve to relativize or "banalize" the Final Solution.[20]

If the Father Pierre–Roger Garaudy affair disturbed the French and especially French historians and intellectuals as much as it did, that malaise was attributable in part to a strong sense of déjà vu where the Holocaust denial is concerned. Negationism has erupted in French public life at regular intervals since the late 1940s, when the fascist Maurice Bardèche published *Nuremberg ou la Terre Promise* (1948). In his book Bardèche articulated a number of theses that Garaudy, among other subsequent negationists, has reiterated. These include the claim that the Allies were as culpable of war crimes as the Germans; that the gas chambers were used for disinfection purposes, not for killing Jews; that deaths in the concentration camps were due to food shortages and epidemics; and that the "'solution to the Jewish problem' simply referred to the establishment of ghettos in the East."[21]

But Bardèche was a self-professed fascist and wartime collaborationist and hence not the most reliable source for an objective discussion of Nazi crimes. It required the intervention of a former Socialist, Paul Rassinier, to launch negationism along the path it has followed in France ever since.

Beginning his career as a member of the Communist Party in the 1920s, Rassinier was excluded from the Party in 1932 and quickly became a functionary in the Socialist Party. Resolutely pacifist even when other Socialists had changed their views as a result of the Nazi threat, Rassinier was an ardent supporter of the Munich Accords. When war came, Rassinier, unlike many of his fellow pacifist Socialists, joined the Resistance. Arrested by the Gestapo in November 1943, Rassinier was tortured and deported to Buchenwald and then to the underground factory at Dora, where working conditions were reputedly among the worst. After the Liberation, Rassinier returned to France and served briefly as a Socialist deputy before veering to the right.[22]

As Pierre Vidal-Naquet explains in his preface to Florent Brayard's recent study of Rassinier, two things are particularly striking about Rassinier's writings on the camps and on the Holocaust itself. The first is that the horrors of the concentration camps were, according to Rassinier, fundamentally attributable not to the ss members who ran them (and with whom Rassinier maintained good relations) but to the nefarious prisoners who had insinuated themselves into positions of authority within the system. Second, Rassinier's negationism emerged only gradually over several years and through the publication of a series of books. In *Le Mensonge d'Ulysse* (1950), for example, Rassinier admits the existence of the gas chambers but argues they were run by a few crazed ss members and those at the top of the prisoners' hierarchy. But by the time of the publication of *Le Véritable Procès Eichmann* (1962) and *Le Drame des Juifs européens*, Rassinier had, as Vidal-Naquet remarks, "gone to the limits of negationism," citing as primary evidence for these views his own experience of the camps.[23]

In his writings during the cold war years, Rassinier, like other negationists, revealed himself to be an obsessive anti-Semite. The Jews, he argued, and not the Nazis were responsible for starting the war, and in the cold war years they would soon be responsible for another war as well. Now on the extreme right, Rassinier contributed to postwar reactionary reviews like *Rivarol* and published his books with presses like Maurice Bardèche's Les Sept Couleurs. A vehement opponent of Israel at the end of his life, Rassinier died just after the Six-Day War in 1967.

While the reasons for Rassinier's turn to negationism, especially given his Socialist and *résistant* past, are of psychological interest (Brayard, for one, attributes it to his profound sense of guilt over having survived, and indeed thrived, while interned in the concentration camps), it is precisely his left-wing origins that makes him a figure of particular interest in the long and sordid history of French negationism. For in the next scandalous eruption of negationism in France, which followed the publication in *Le Monde* in December 1978 of negationist articles by Robert Faurisson, what surprised and shocked many was that Faurisson's most vociferous supporters came not from the extreme right but the extreme left, and specifically from the disaffected Trotskyists of La Vieille Taupe. Moreover, when Faurisson's book defending his negationist claims was published in 1980 by La Vieille Taupe, it was prefaced by none other than the distinguished American linguist and leftist activist Noam Chomsky.[24] I shall return to Chomsky's role in the affair shortly.

Unlike Paul Rassinier or, later, Roger Garaudy, Faurisson was neither a concentration camp survivor nor a political activist. He was instead a professor of French literature, first in a girls' high school in Vichy (where, appropriately enough, he now resides) and later at the University of Lyons II, where he served as a lecturer in twentieth-century French literature. In statements made in the hagiographic account of his life written by François Brigneau, Faurisson also claims not to be, or ever to have been, pro-Nazi or anti-Semitic.[25] In fact Faurisson states that in his youth during the Occupation he was staunchly *résistant* and anti-German. Teased by his classmates for being pro-English (Faurisson's mother was British), the young Robert was punished for carving "Death to Laval" on his desk, and he claims as well to have been in favor of the harshest punishments for collaborators.

But it was also during the war, or at least at the Liberation, that Faurisson supposedly developed sympathy for the sufferings of France's erstwhile enemies, the Germans, and became suspicious of Allied justice and the "myths" the Allies generated concerning the conflict. Attending in person the trial of a *milicien* after the war, Faurisson claims to have witnessed firsthand the inequities of the "victor's justice." Henceforth the "justice of Nuremberg" would make him "nauseous."

According to his own account, Faurisson did not become interested in the Holocaust or begin to entertain doubts about its occurrence until he read Rassinier in 1960. This was followed by years of reflection and arduous research, culminating in the "good news to humanity"—that the Holocaust was a hoax—which he announced in the pages of *Le Monde* in 1978.

In his book on Rassinier, Brayard carefully dismantles what he describes as Faurisson's "novel of origins"—that is, his claims concerning his early political views and the chronology of his "enlightenment" where the Holocaust is concerned. Brayard notes that Faurisson happened to attend high school in Paris in the late 1940s with Pierre Vidal-Naquet and others and that the latters' testimony confirms that Faurisson was already avowedly pro-Nazi and anti-Semitic. Brayard also cites evidence, drawn from Faurisson's own version of events, that Faurisson was well aware of Rassinier and his negationist theses, as well as those in the work of Maurice Bardèche, long before 1960.

If Faurisson's fallacious account of his past and his conversion to negationism calls his credibility into question, it is, curiously, his approach as a literary critic that accurately foreshadows key features of his later "methodology" as a negationist. Indeed, Faurisson achieved his first notoriety not in revealing "the truth" where the Holocaust was concerned but in disclosing the "real meaning" of Arthur Rimbaud's famous poem "Voyelles." In an essay published anonymously in 1961 in the literary review *Bizarre*, Faurisson offered his analysis under the provocative title "A-t-on lu Rimbaud?" Faurisson claimed that several generations of literary critics had completely misinterpreted the poem. In reality Rimbaud's celebrated poem was little more than a disguised erotic fantasy of an adolescent school boy dreaming of women. According to Faurisson's analysis, the letters *A* and *U*, for example, were inverted figures of the female genitalia and hair respectively, while the letter *E* figured a woman's breasts, tilted upright. As one critic commenting on Faurisson's reading explained, it was precisely because of the erotic nature of his analysis that he wished to keep his identity a secret. He did not wish his students back at the girls' high school at Vichy grinning knowingly at him while he delivered his lectures.

Remarkably, the publication of "A-t-on lu Rimbaud?" created quite a stir in Parisian literary circles. In the pages of leading reviews including *Les Temps Modernes*, the *Nouvelle Revue Française*, *Combat*, *L'Express*, and many others, prominent literary critics responded to Faurisson, often favorably. Luminaries including André Breton and Antoine Adam praised "A-t-on lu Rimbaud?" for its originality.[26]

Encouraged by his success, Faurisson followed his study of "Voyelles" with similar "definitive" readings of Gérard de Nerval's *Chimères* and Lautréamont's *Les Chants de Maldoror*. In both cases, he claimed to overturn generations of faulty interpretations to get at "the truth" of the works in question and, as was the case with his reading of Rimbaud's poem, provocatively entitled his reading of Lautréamont *A-t-on lu Lautréamont?* As these titles imply, all previous interpretations of the literary works in question are, according to Faurisson, no more than "mystifications," a term that would recur with a much more ominous meaning in the author's subsequent writings on the Holocaust. It is Faurisson's intention, as Brayard suggests, not just to challenge previous interpretations but to bury them, since, as Faurisson affirms, "Every text has only one meaning or it has no meaning at all."[27] Moreover, the method is "totalitarian," Brayard continues, in the sense that where Faurisson chooses to apply it, there is no meaning possible other than the one that he imposes. Faurisson's disdain for all previous readings and interpretations and all "external" considerations is evident in the description in *A-t-on lu Lautréamont?* of his own "radical" methodology:

Introduction

The method that we constrain ourselves to adhere to is of an aus-tere simplicity. This method will appear forbidding to more than one reader. It consists in taking the attitude of a profanator who considers it his obligation to understand everything about a work concerning which he knows nothing, beginning with the name of the author and the historical period during which the work was written. The method consists in finding the meaning of the word in the sentence, the meaning of the sentence in the page, the page in the book or poem, without recourse to biography, bibliography, or "sources," without reference to historical considerations, without concerning oneself with the author's declarations concerning his own work, without the assistance of other works, without any sup-port other than dictionaries of the French language—and these to be consulted with suspicion. Whether the work in question is poetry or prose, it must be considered by itself, for itself, naked, raw, and . . . only at the exact level of the text itself."[28]

As his lengthy discourse on his methodology suggests, there is ultimately for Faurisson no authority, no *cogito*, other than himself, and no frame of reference or epistomological principles to which he ultimately holds himself accountable. Moreover, as "profanator" it is his job to strip the work of its sacred meaning just as one scours a dirty pot or pan. It is not surprising that Faurisson's students referred to his approach as the "Ajax method."[29]

The arbitrariness of Faurisson's "method," as well as his willingness to violate his own principles when it suits his purposes, becomes abundantly clear when the "method" is applied to reading the Holocaust. In *Assassins of Mem-ory*, Vidal-Naquet implicitly debunks many of Faurisson's "purist" pretensions in his discussion of the tactics of French negationists and of Faurisson in particular. The negationist strategy is in fact riddled with prejudicial presuppositions, the arbitrary inclusion or dismissal of evidence, deliberately faulty historical contextualization, and so on. As summarized by Vidal-Naquet, the "analytic principles" followed by the negationists are as follows:

1. Any direct testimony by a Jew is a lie or a fantasy by definition.

2. Any document dating from before the Liberation is to be treated as a forgery or a rumor.

3. Any document containing firsthand information on Nazi methods—for example, those testimonies concerning the Warsaw ghetto—either is a forgery or has been tampered with.

4. Any Nazi "coded" document—that is, using euphemisms for practices associated with the extermination of Jews—is to be interpreted in its strictly literal meaning, whereas any document speaking plainly of the genocide is to be ignored or "underinterpreted."

5. Any Nazi testimony dating from after the war is to be considered as obtained under torture or other forms of coercion.

6. An enormous amount of pseudotechnical evidence is marshaled to confirm the impossibility of the existence and functioning of the gas chambers.

7. Any complementary evidence that would make the Holocaust more plausible in historical and evolutionary terms—such as the Nazi euthanasia of the mentally ill or the activities of the Einsatzgruppen—is either "unacknowledged or falsified."[30]

As noted earlier, when the scandal erupted following the publication of Faurisson's negationist claims, public consternation and shock were less attributable to doubts about the Holocaust that Faurisson may have sown than to the support that he garnered on the far left. Chomsky's preface to Faurisson's *Mémoire en défense* was preceded by a 1979 petition signed by Chomsky that described Faurisson as a "respected professor of twentieth-century French literature and document criticism" and called for an end to the "vicious campaign of harassment, intimidation, slander and physical violence" to which he had been subject following his pronouncements concerning the Holocaust.[31] The petition also called on university and government officials to guarantee Faurisson's right to "academic freedom" and free access to "public libraries and archives."[32] What the petition did not explain was that the archives in question were housed in the Centre de Documentation Juive in Paris. Set up to preserve the memory and document the history of the Holocaust, the Centre de Documentation Juive had allowed Faurisson free access to its archives until his purpose in carrying out his research had become all too clear.

Chomsky's preface to *Mémoire en défense* follows much the same line of reasoning as the 1979 petition. It defends Faurisson's right to "free speech" and attacks many members of the French intelligentsia for their lack of respect for the "facts" and for "reason" both in their desire to gag Faurisson and in their misrepresentation and denunciation of the petition Chomsky had signed. Chomsky goes on to assert that no such violation of civil rights in this context would occur in the United States, and he concludes by noting that the evidence he has seen suggests that Faurisson is not a rabid anti-Semite or pro-Nazi zealot but "a sort of apolitical liberal." It was this statement, perhaps more than his attacks on French intellectuals in general, that genuinely outraged many.[33]

Before turning to French extreme left-wing support for Faurisson's negationism, which brings us full circle to the Roger Garaudy–Father Pierre affair in the 1990s—and to the subject of Alain Finkielkraut's *The Future of a Negation*—it is important to consider the denouement of the Faurisson affair and one final issue it foregrounded.

In May–June 1981, Faurisson stood trial in Paris on three separate charges. The first was a slander charge, brought by the distinguished historian Léon Poliakov, whom Faurisson had accused of falsifying his sources vis-à-vis evidence of the gassing of the Jews. The second charge concerned the responsibility of the historian. Faurisson was accused of willfully distorting history in violation of article 382 of the civil code. The final charge was that of incitement to racial hatred, a charge brought against Faurisson for anti-Semitic comments he made on French radio in claiming that the lie of the Holocaust had been exploited by the State of Israel to "swindle" money from Germany and victimize the German and Palestinian people.[34]

Of the three charges, the most troubling from a legal, historical, and indeed historiographical point of view is the second one. In effect, in spite of efforts to avoid the problem, the court was asked to pass judgment on a version of history, a procedure fraught with danger, as the various court decisions involving crimes against humanity charges against Paul Touvier would demonstrate in the 1990s.[35] From a historical and historiographical perspective, the problem is that in refuting negationist arguments and interpretations of the evidence, the historian engages with them, thereby giving their claims an aura of respectability as well as a legitimacy they do not merit. As Vidal-Naquet observes: "A dialogue between two parties, even if they are adversaries, presupposes a common ground, a common respect—in this case for truth. But with the 'revisionists,' such ground does not exist." To underscore the absurdity of this type of exchange, Vidal-Naquet wonders if one could "conceive of an astrophysicist entering into a dialogue with a 'researcher' claiming that the moon is made of Roquefort cheese."[36] As Charles Korman has suggested recently in the context of the Roger Garaudy–Father Pierre affair: "Jurists and historians make a mistake in playing along with the negationists. One should not speak of History with them, nor condemn them in the name of History, but speak instead of racism and condemn them for that. A negationist is simply someone who incites to racism."[37]

If racism and a visceral anti-Semitism account for extreme right-wing support for the negationists—and young neofascists showed up at Faurisson's trial to, among other things, snicker at the gruesome details of the gassings[38]—what, finally, explains the support Faurisson received from Pierre Guillaume, Serge Thion, and other radical leftists associated with La Vieille Taupe? As the Roger Garaudy–Father Pierre affair confirms, that support continues today, so much so that, according to Taguieff, the distinctive trait of French negationism as opposed to that of other countries is its "anchorage" on the extreme left among "anarcho-communists" of the "Trotskyist tendency."[39] It is this seemingly paradoxical phenomenon that Alain Finkielkraut set out to explain in 1982 with the publication of *The Future of a Negation*.

Finkielkraut was, first of all, no stranger to anti-Semitism or anti-Zionism, nor for that matter was he unfamiliar with the excesses of post "sixty-eight" radical left-wing thinking in France. The son of Polish Jews (his father, who had been deported to Auschwitz, survived), Finkielkraut had already meditated on Jewish identity and the implications of the Holocaust in *Le Juif imaginaire* (1980). A short while after the publication of *The Future of an Illusion*, he would write on anti-Zionist and anti-Israeli sentiment in *La Réprobation d'Israël* (1983). Initially a committed "sixty-eight" activist, Finkielkraut abandoned his studies as the student movement gained momentum and participated actively in the political upheavals. He then renounced his radical stance after a year and returned to school to finish his degree.[40]

In accounting for left-wing support for Faurisson in *The Future of a Negation*, Finkielkraut focuses his attention initially not on the views of figures like Guillaume and Thion in the 1970s and 1980s but on the attitudes of many prominent Socialists at the time of the Dreyfus affair. These attitudes, he believes, set the stage for the negationism to come. Finkielkraut notes that at the time of the affair, the renowned German Socialist leader Wilhelm Liebknecht went on record, first in Germany and then in the pages of *Action Française*, denouncing the Dreyfusards and proclaiming Dreyfus's guilt. Moreover, the possibility that he might be innocent was for Liebknecht logically impossible. As Finkielkraut explains, in Liebknecht's view the ruling class had only one enemy, the proletariat, and if the former wished to punish one of its own, the wealthy bourgeois officer Dreyfus, it must have had a good reason—he had to be guilty. While the logic employed by Liebknecht is not overtly anti-Semitic, it is implicitly so to the extent that Jews were associated with capital and thereby implicated in the abuses of the latter in the suppression of the working class.

So how does this fin de siècle leftist anti-Dreyfusard logic come to permeate the thinking of Guillaume and his colleagues at La Vieille Taupe? The intervening eight decades and the momentous events that transpired during those years must certainly have influenced the thinking even of a group of disaffected and isolated radicals. Finkielkraut's response is that they did and did not. The great events and ideological struggles are taken into account by Guillaume and his colleagues, but they are subsumed in the same paranoid logic that informed Liebknecht's critique of the Dreyfus affair. For the "anarcho-communists" of La Vieille Taupe, capital embodied in the Western democracies is still the arch enemy in the class struggle, to be joined in this century by the corrupt Stalinism of the Soviet Bloc. But where does that leave fascism—and Nazism in particular? Following the traditional Marxist analysis, Nazism was simply a hypertrophied form of capitalism that evolved as a bulwark against the threat posed by the proletariat. Accordingly, very little

separates the three systems in question, since all are ultimately geared to suppress the revolution of the workers and
the downtrodden to the benefit of capital.

But in a particularly diabolical manipulation designed to
dupe the workers as to who their real enemies were, the
West, with the support of the Soviets, sought to demonize
the Nazis, to make *them* the embodiment of all evil. And the
best way to accomplish this aim was to point to the Holocaust, the quintessentially evil event that set the Nazis completely apart from those who had struggled against them.

So the Holocaust, as Finkielkraut explains, was the stick-
ing point in the logic of history espoused by La Vieille
Taupe: it was quite simply a stumbling block that had to
be removed at all costs. When Faurisson appeared with his
voluminous "evidence," he provided Guillaume and his colleagues not only with a means of removing the obstacle they
had not previously been able to overcome but also with a
cause that has served as their rallying cry ever since.

In the wake of the Roger Garaudy–Father Pierre affair,
Finkielkraut was asked to comment on the implications of
this latest episode of negationism in the pages of *L'Evenement
du jeudi*. Situating the French version of the Holocaust denial in a broader historical context, Finkielkraut noted sadly
that our century is "the century of negation" and explained:
"History has become the theater of Reason. No distance
must remain between the real and the 'rational.' But what
does one do with facts that do not coincide with the supposed logic of History? The simplest thing is to deny them."[41]
If history now functions in this fashion, then *The Future of
a Negation* should be read not only as a means of understanding negations past but, as its title implies, of future
negations as well.

RICHARD J. GOLSAN

He filled the glasses and raised his own glass by the stem.

"What shall it be this time?" he said, still with the same faint suggestion of irony. "To the confusion of the Thought Police? To the death of Big Brother? To humanity? To the future?"

"To the past," said Winston.

"The past is more important," agreed O'Brien gravely.

GEORGE ORWELL, 1984

Prologue
Facts Are Not Stubborn

1984: a different time when truth no longer exists: everything can be true, and—in a triumph of power over destiny itself—no act is irremediable, no trace is indelible; what has been done can always be undone. "If the Party could thrust its hand into the past and say of this or that event, *it never happened*—that, surely, was more terrifying than mere torture and death."

Everyone knows the places where this other time has come to pass; we live in that half of Europe exempt from its reign. Disenchanted as most of us are with our old dreams of revolution, we are well aware of this privilege—and its fragility.

Yet when one man thrust his fist into the past and, referring to the Nazi gas chambers, exclaimed *it never happened*, almost no one recognized him as the emulator of Big Brother. In the eyes of the most implacable adversaries of all systems of domination, he was even a martyr of repression, a victim of censorship. Hatred for power gained him not enemies but sympathizers.

This was possible because we abhor totalitarianism without, however, embracing the values that are intolerable to the totalitarian State. Indeed, we must reverse Lenin's famous proposition. In the world in which we live, facts are not stubborn; facts are precarious, docile, malleable. They can be adapted to suit any and every purpose, or bent to comply with the dictates of dogma, or swallowed up in the soft belly of public opinion. Beneath its facade as an isolated event or a trivial news item, the attempted revision of the

Prologue

Nazi genocide of the Jews reveals an allergy to the event and the crisis of truth that plague our culture.

In *1984*, Orwell describes the violent death of values whose gentle, painless, nontotalitarian evaporation we are experiencing today. Without there being only a single party, and without any violation of our fundamental liberties, facts are being undone; what is real is being made unreal. My intent: to study the modalities of this obliteration by examining the question of the genocide of the Jews.

I

The Worker, Martyr, and Savior

"For whom are you working, Mr. Faurisson?" It was on radio station Europe I, on 19 December 1980, to be precise. A few minutes of air time on Ivan Levaï's broadcast marked the crowning point of the doggedness of the professor who for several years had been applying himself to proving the nonexistence of the gas chambers in the Nazi concentration camps. He had been offered an extraordinary opportunity to share his discovery with the silent majority of French people. Admittedly the harm was almost already done: the denial of the genocide had just made its way into the news and was causing quite a stir. This thesis, which was no longer confidential but not yet totally public, was suddenly catapulted to the height (or depth) of scandal. And this, we recall, thanks to Noam Chomsky's preface on the theme of freedom of expression, which he had written for the most recent of Mr. Faurisson's books, *Mémoire en défense*. Ivan Levaï, who wanted to provide proof that it was wrong to worry and that Faurisson could indeed speak freely, was at the same time almost angered by his own initiative. He felt caught in a trap, driven in spite of himself to offer an ideal tribune to his interlocutor. To denounce a lie is to nourish it with the energy one devotes to it, and the slightest comment that it inspires one to make, no matter what its pertinence, is an offering for which it can be grateful. Completely focused on the value to be rescued, one overlooks the inexorable workings of fashion, the sovereign form that establishes that equivalence of the pro and the con, that turns yes and no into two identical modalities of the *echo*. In the communication system that is ours today, all controversy works to the benefit of the adversary. However justified the battle might be, the enemy always draws the advantage, for in accordance with the bizarre rules of this war, the enemy grows stronger with each blow he receives.

Disturbed by this ambiguity, conflicted by two certainties (that of depriving absolute liberalism of its major argument and that of being used himself), Ivan Levaï intended at the very least to show that he was not fooled, that he knew with whom he was dealing. "For whom are you working?" The journalist was aiming his question beyond Faurisson, from whom he was expecting no sensational confession, addressing it instead to his listeners, to arouse their suspicions and to tell them, in so many words, not to take seriously the lie they were being fed. In short, the question itself secretly revealed its own answer: Faurisson was working for Hitler. He puts so much effort into erasing from history the annihilation of six million Jews, he exercises such dogged determination in burying the crime in accordance with the explicit wishes of those who crafted it that one is led to the obvious and unavoidable conclusion: Faurisson worships the Third Reich, and he cloaks this forbidden devotion in the dazzling austerity of a hodgepodge of figures and references; he dresses up his nostalgia in the rigor of scientific investigation just as the new right is giving a face-lift to the discredited fantasies of racial purity and Aryan supremacy in order to make them more presentable.[1]

If only this were the case. Everything would be in order. Heart on the left; money on the right; on the extreme right, the beast. And since my immediate reaction was the same as theirs, I understand those people working to flush out the apologetic project that underlies a phony erudition and the appearance of objectivity. Indeed, what could be more natural than to seek a connection between the technicians of extermination and the so-called revisionists? When all is said and done, two prodigious innovations will have to be credited expressly to the twentieth century: genocide and its demystification, the scientific capability to finish off the existence of certain human groups, coupled with the aptitude for erasing their deaths. That said, there is such *continuity* between these projects that it is both legitimate and inevitable for one to infer the *complicity* of their authors.

One must not, however, yield to what seems obvious: those who committed the massacres and those who would expunge the record are not interchangeable. Levaï, in his anger, was only half right: "revisionism" is a fiction that reveals nothing if not the mentality of those who propagate it, but it is not solely a neo-Nazi fiction.[2] If the fanatical admirers of the ss uniform were the only ones seeking to rehabilitate Hitler, if they had the monopoly on trivialization, there would be no "affair." Vigilance would suffice; reflection would be optional. The thing is, Faurisson is not content to draw followers only from the pool where one would expect him to: the proselytes of negation do not all decorate their bedroom walls with gigantic swastikas or portraits of the Führer, not by a long shot. For every Maurice Bardèche, for every Marc Frederiksen, there are countless anti-Nazis now convinced that the gas chambers are a hoax or, in any case, an unverifiable rumor![3]

It is true that, Nazi or not, this "new history" does not exactly make one want to delve into the particulars of the matter. Faced with a delirium that no longer says "Everything Jewish is evil," nor even "Everything evil is Jewish," but "The Jews invented the evil that the world is supposed to have committed," one feels as if one has been projected into a nightmare; and one's immediate, irresistible response is that of disgust and indignation. Because, if for a second, one takes seriously the "good word" of the revisionists, the limits of Jewish malfeasance must once again be extended.

What are the *Protocols of the Elders of Zion* compared to the deception of the gas chambers? What is a satanic plot to gain control of the world compared to the skill required of a living people to substantiate the lie of its extermination and to reap enormous benefit from it? Compared to Faurisson's Zionists, the exilarchs of the *Protocols* are timid precursors, and their stratagems almost innocent teasing. In the final analysis, revision of the genocide conjures up a brand new devil next to whom the most demonic figures engendered by superstition and fear look like small-time hoodlums, petty hooligans.

And yet rage is a luxury we cannot afford. Within these revisionist ramblings is something that forces us to think: a violence wrought on our most firmly rooted certainties, an unbearable paradox that compels us to reflect, that establishes—against our will—the absolute necessity of an act of intelligence. Negation cannot be put down to the evil that it strives to excuse or, even better, to abolish: its discourse exceeds the bounds of the ideology to which it is ascribed, and its followers do not fit the image that the general public has of them. Others besides fascists are humming or broadcasting "the insidious tune of the genocide problem."[4] We must solve the enigma of this discrepancy.

"DOWN WITH LIEBKNECHT!"

The longer this affair is over, the clearer it becomes that it will never be over. Charles Péguy

In December 1899, the first general congress of Socialists took place in Paris. Each in a multitude of small parties still claimed to have the monopoly on revolutionary truth. All of them, however—the Guesdists of the French workers' party, the Blanquists, the Possibilists, the *allemanistes*,

and the independents united behind Jean Jaurès and behind
René Vivani—had agreed to answer the call.[5] Was this a step
toward unity? On the contrary: these were times for settling scores or even for excommunications. A crucial problem arose concerning the future of the revolution in France.
Millerand—a Socialist—had just agreed to be Minister of
Commerce in the Waldeck-Rousseau cabinet. And as if to
make this collaboration even more sacrilegious, he sat on
this government along with General de Gallifet, the sadly
notorious "butcher" of the Commune. Could a Socialist participate in bourgeois power without betraying his own principles? For four days running, in the Salle Jappy, orators
of various persuasions confronted one another in stormy
debate. When it was Jules Guesde's turn at the tribune, the
"ministerials" braced themselves for a harsh attack. For some
time now, the "drill sergeant" of the workers' movement had
been the very incarnation of doctrinal rigidity in the face of
the reformists' willingness to compromise. And right from
the start, he unleashed himself against what he considered to
be an unspeakable betrayal. His rivalry with Jaurès further
roused his eloquence. To add the weight of the Last Judgment to the indictment he was delivering with such grandil-
oquence, Guesde invoked the patronage of the great figures
of socialism and protested in the name of those foreign revolutionaries who were so many tutelary gods: Schoenlank,
Bebel, Liebknecht.

A single anonymous voice interrupted him: "Down with
Liebknecht!" Speechless with amazement for several sec-
onds, the crowd then let out a furious roar. By insulting
the patriarch of German social democracy, the unknown
agitator had just committed the most irreparable of crimes.
"Imagine a man in Notre Dame, at the moment when all
heads are turned to the Holy Sacrament, shouting 'Down
with God!' and you will have some idea of the initial horror,

followed by anger, on the faces of the Guesdists. In the blink
of an eye, the tribune was overrun."[6] The heretic was pointed
out, and after a few moments of chaotic, tumultuous agitation, he was asked to justify his behavior. But scarcely could
he get two words out, for the whole hall, supercharged with
emotion, was calling for his expulsion. This was immediately
put to a vote and passed by a majority. The president-citizen,
traumatized by the scandal, proposed to vote a show of
sympathy for German democracy and "its venerable dean,
Liebknecht." The applause was unanimous. Part of the hall
began to sing the *International*, as if to celebrate the unity
regained by banishing the culprit and to purify socialism of
the wound inflicted upon it by his outburst. Then everything
calmed down, and Jules Guesde was able take up his speech
where he had left off. They had punished "the man who
dared to spit on the beard of the gods."[7]

The man's name was Joindy, and if he had braved the
militants' indignation in just this way, he had done so—as
he unsuccessfully tried so hard to explain—in the name of
the recent battle against the reaction linked to anti-Semitism.
In toppling the idol, he had no intention of provoking a
schism; he simply wanted to speak out against the heinous
sentiments that Wilhelm Liebknecht, in a series of articles
published by *Die Fackel* and translated in *L'Action française*,
had just expressed in regard to Dreyfusism.

For the great revolutionary from across the Rhine, Dreyfus could not be innocent. Such a hypothesis was logically
absurd. "Is it realistic, is it admissible that a French officer
from a very influential family be condemned for a crime of
high treason that he did not commit and remain locked up
for five long years?" In other words, having only a single
adversary—the proletariat—the ruling class reserves its dirty
tricks exclusively for that lone adversary: the rich are never
punished except for very good reasons. Injustice arises from

war, and why would the bourgeoisie wage war against her own children? In capitalist society, law shields and strengthens exploitation, and Dreyfus was never part of the world of the exploited. He therefore deserves his punishment. Rest assured: there is nothing arbitrary in his trial and his condemnation, in his banishment to Devil's Island. It is not facts but rather the logic of history, namely the class struggle, that counts as proof. There is an implacable coherence of events, and if a doubt arises, if reality lags behind, rambles, or takes some unexpected turns, it is suspicion that is to blame, for the logic of history cannot possibly be at fault. As we know, this type of reasoning would meet with far-reaching acceptance. Still uncommon with the left of that era, it triumphed on the right, among the followers of biological determinism. "That Dreyfus is capable of betrayal is a conclusion I draw from his race," said Maurice Barrès with the haughtiness of someone who has tamed history. By deducing *from his class* that Dreyfus could not be innocent, Liebknecht offered the revolutionary variant of the same demonstration. Having adopted, like Barrès, a philosophy of movement or evolution (*devenir*), he could treat contradictors with the same disdainful indifference and assign only a secondary role of *confirmation* to judiciary facts.

With their exposure in France in the nationalist press, these ideas were beginning to gain recognition. But they were not enough to discredit Liebknecht in the eyes of the majority of Socialists. His immense reputation could not be sullied by what appeared to be, at worst, excessive rigorism. And besides, wasn't the case of Millerand a warning to beware of the opposite extreme? Shouldn't revolutionary vigilance be exercised first against the apostles of compromise and class collaboration? One began by diverting the workers from their essential objectives and polarizing them over a problem that was internal to the enemy class, and one gradually ended up curbing, then abandoning, the ambitions of socialism. Instead of saving one's strength for decisive, liberating action, one became obsessed with the misfortune of an individual, and that was how one progressively became the guarantor of the same world that one had originally set out to destroy. For Guesde, as for Vaillant, the worm of "ministerialism" was in the fruit of Dreyfusism. In retrospect, Millerand's joining a bourgeois cabinet shed a light of betrayal on the battle for truth and for the salvation of one man. To become involved in the conflicts of the society that needed to be destroyed was to agree in advance to cooperate in running it.

All it took was that the Socialist Party leave its class turf fragmentarily; all it took was that, one day, it form a first alliance with a fraction of the bourgeoisie for it to threaten to slide all the way down this slippery slope. For the purposes of an act of justice and individual reparation, it got mixed up with the enemy class, and now here it was dragged into running a common government with that class.[8]

The majority of Socialists thus rediscovered the principle that had been their own at the time of the publication of *J'accuse*: this is no concern of ours! No need to choose between the "*justiciards*" and "*patriotards*," the extremists on either side of the Dreyfus question, for the revolution incumbent upon us will be achievable to the extent that we remain true to ourselves.

Even Fernand Pelloutier, in his blanket opposition to Guesde's centralism and with his primary focus on destruction of the State, agreed with his old adversary on this negative requirement: they needed to stay out of the debate that was ripping the country apart. A friend of Bernard-Lazare, Pelloutier the anarcho-syndicalist recognized Dreyfus's innocence and rose up against the barbarity of his judges.[9]

But Pelloutier was no less adamant in urging the people "to look with increasing detachment upon the fierce contests that appeal to the public's strength" and to save themselves "for the time when the people will have force enough to make the whole capitalist edifice come tumbling down."[10]

In an atmosphere such as this, poor Joindy's eviction is more easily understood: Liebknecht went farther than the other revolutionaries since he slipped from nonintervention to anti-Dreyfusism, but the same mode of thought was at work. The venerated dean was perhaps excessive, but he was not beyond the bounds of the dominant philosophy.

What role, if any, did anti-Semitism play in this? It most certainly had its part in an era when capital and Jewish capital were frequently regarded as one and the same. It is also true that a number of Socialists viewed the anti-Jewish revolts with a sort of benevolent consideration—that of a father who watches intently and sees in his child the precocious signs of thought, the promise of a great intellect. Anti-Semitism was only a beginning, a rich and decisive beginning that was a training ground where fighting against a secondary enemy was the means of preparing for the ultimate battle against the principal one.

It would be wrong to ascribe to the archaism of prejudice an attitude that was actually in keeping with revolutionary logic. It is not possible to excuse the doctrine by situating outside the domain of socialist ideology the gibes against the republic or the scorn for the notion of inviolable rights. It was not so much opportunism as it was intransigence that led the Socialists to put themselves above the fray and simply keep score. No doubt some of them pandered to the instincts of the crowd in order to keep their seats as deputies; others, with more influence, maintained that in trying to correct an injustice created in a capitalist society (if an abuse has truly been committed) *one overlooks the essence in favor of*

the accident, one disregards the injustice that this society itself represents. To discredit anti-Dreyfusard France was to
reconfirm liberal France, whereas the trained eye of the revolutionary was supposed to be able to recognize this confrontation as a power struggle between two clans of the
bourgeoisie. For example, Guesde could censure anti-Semitic superstitions and at the same time glorify the noble cause
of proletarian impassiveness. The contradiction was only an
apparent one: the Socialists were assigning themselves the
task of liquidating the old world and not of becoming actively involved within it, whether it be to play up to or to
reform its most vile beliefs.

THE TWO MESSIANISMS

France, as we know—and it is even one of its amusing particularities—discovered how to raise the concepts of right and
left to the height of metaphysical categories. And to some
extent, we owe this incredible advancement to the Dreyfus
affair. Indeed, two blocs gradually emerged: the party of the
republic was reconstituted in opposition to the common enemy, but beyond democracy and Caesarism, it was truth and
justice that clashed with the natural alliance of racism and
iniquity. And traces of this battle can still be found in the way
we envision politics today and in the importance we attach
to its fundamental division. Left and right: these are the two
terms that our lay society will probably never manage to
secularize. Within this dualism is an inexhaustible transcendence, an enigmatic surplus of sentiment over sense; try as
we might, we fail to bring these words under our control;
they slip past their literal meaning and perpetually designate
more than the contrast between two ways of managing the
economy or two visions of society. Supposing even that the
systems become closer to one another and that the discourse

on both sides grows increasingly similar, the opposition will remain irreducible, and Manichaeism, a supreme paradox, will survive up to the point of homogeneity. Almost everyone will invoke the same values of progress, growth, and social justice, but behind this consensus, absolutism and the citizen's right will carry on their battle—a persistent echo of the trial that inflamed all of France more than a century ago.[11]

This reference, so rewarding for the left, nevertheless overlooks a significant fact: the isolation of Jaurès and the practically unanimous and constant reticence of the other leaders of the worker-power movement to mobilize for Dreyfus. Despite his talents as an orator, Jaurès was able to win over only a minority of Socialists (our unfortunate Joindy among them) for the defense of the prisoner of Devil's Island. And for good reason: it was not just a strategy, a mood, a temperament that he was opposing to the strict doctrinarians of "class strugglism"—it was, under the same name of revolution, *another messianism*. Jaurès, who was uncompromising on the matter of radicality, simply refused to think that future revolution could arise out of absolute deprivation. Such discourse fell on deaf ears among the modern-day riders of the apocalypse who painted capitalism as the apotheosis of alienation, the culminating point of the subjugation of man. From the point of view of canonical socialism, only a social category on the level of a "universal scandal," a category that could be held out as "the notorious crime of all of society," will end oppression for all through its own liberation. In the *suffering* of the proletariat, there is reconciliation of the particular and the universal, the emancipation of a class and that of all of humanity. Consequently, the more misery the workers have to endure, the closer the day of reckoning becomes. The more corruption there is in the existing world, "the greater will be the plenitude of ultimate perfection and liberation in the world to come."[12] According to the schema of alienation, every aggravation of servitude rebounds against the masters, reinforces the imminence of their collapse, and accelerates the coming of the Kingdom. Liberty has its crosses to bear: the times are ripe; the proletariat can accomplish its work once it is stripped of all rights, divested of all guarantees, and plunged into the historical and social void.

Jaurès did not practice this logic of the worst case. In fact he was not afraid to fight against it, even in Marx himself, in whom he noted a "sort of joy tinged with a bit of dialectical mysticalness at observing the crushing forces that weigh upon the proletarians." And he concluded, "Marx imagines the modern emancipation movement in a Hegelian transposition of Christianity."[13] In order to lift up all men, didn't the Christian God have to descend to the depths of suffering humanity? The proletariat, the "modern Savior," will follow the same itinerary to arrive at the same result, albeit on this earth.

He whom one tends to dismiss too easily as merely a noble orator did not write *Les Preuves* in an irrational rush of compassion. Jaurès became a Dreyfusard because he deliberately interpreted everything in a contrary fashion. Instead of rejoicing over the corruptions of capitalism, he worried about them; instead of slamming the values of this life as invalid, he judged certain ones to be essential to the very idea of civilization. And in this way, he himself determined the philosophical meaning of his fight: to remove the idea of revolution from its apocalyptic model, to separate socialism from all Christian references. Let us not do away with the past; distress and impoverishment are not what qualify the proletariat to save the world.

Are the rights of man being subjected to ridicule? This is no cause for celebration. For these rights constitute that part of humanity already established—the fundamental, fragile patrimony that the proletariat is quite naturally duty bound to protect and affirm. "Life does not abolish the past: it takes control of it. Revolution is not a rupture, it is a conquest."[14]

Is the bourgeoisie exposing its wounds, admitting its inherent abjection? Those who pin the kingdom of liberated humanity on the degradation of living society will have wasted their time and efforts. For the debasement of the existing world is not a promise: far from heralding deliverance, degradation delays it and renders it uncertain.

He knew that in the end, bourgeois ignominies are practiced against woeful humanity, common humanity, and that what is therefore compromised in the end is the very heritage of future socialism, of the next socialism. . . . He knew that these ignominies are always brought to bear on living people and that if they seem to justify certain nonliving formulas, they run the risk of doing irremediable damage to humanity itself.[15]

And if one now wonders who in the Socialist circle had the greater impact on succeeding generations, Guesde or Jaurès, the history of the twentieth century compels us to answer: Guesde. Defeated in practice, leftist non-Dreyfusism would survive in people's minds at least as a mode of thought: the logic of equivalence and the principle of all or nothing provided the model for the great leveling of fascism and democracy that would inspire first the communist parties' strategy of "class against class" and then, throughout the 1930s, leftist opposition to the sacred union against Hitler.

ANTICAPITALISM VERSUS ANTIFASCISM: A TRADITION

1935. At that time, a single imperative—and it was a negative one—lent unity to the groups on the extreme left that

were otherwise tearing each other apart with the raging violence of enemy brothers: do not fall into the trap of antifascism. Refuse to give preference to any one capitalist power
over another. Do not choose the wrong adversary; and treat
Hitler, that other imperialist, as an absolute enemy.

One would be naturally inclined to look back on the German-Soviet nonaggression pact as the first great breakup between the extreme left and Stalinism. In fact, the split dates
back to another accord, one concluded in Moscow between
Stalin and Laval in which the two countries agreed to mutual
aid and assistance in case of attack, for a period of five years.
"Mr. Stalin understands and fully approves of the politics
of national defense in which France is engaged in order to
maintain its armed force's ability to ensure its national security." In short, for the revolutionary minorities, the scandal
or decisive break was not Stalin signing with Hitler in 1939
but Stalin signing *against him* four years earlier. This move
entailed "a profound and irreversible change in the very strategy of Western Marxism: *ouvriérisme*, the workers' movement, which saw only "direct and autonomous action by the
international proletariat"[16] as the means to revolution, lost
its status as the essential factor of doctrine and praxis.

"Mr." Stalin: this grotesque combination symbolized the
betrayal. One could regard one's leader as quite the gentle-
man, for Russia had become a country like any other; by
negotiating a military accord with France, it proved over-
whelmingly that it had abandoned the principles of proletarian internationalism for the benefit of its own selfish interest.
Anarchists, syndicalists of *La Révolution prolétarienne*, Pivertists of the sfio,[17] Trotskyites, all sects of anticapitalism were
devastated by such a cynical about-face, by such a quiet
abandoning of revolutionary defeatism. Only because
Stalin's decision left them no other choice did the Communists themselves give up their renunciation of jingoistic

warmongering and their opposition to the military budget increase. They complied out of discipline and not out of conviction. For there was a contradiction between antifascism and revolutionary thought. To mobilize against Hitler was to make national spirit prevail over class spirit and to make the apocalypse of war prevail over that of revolution. Antifascism blurred the fundamental opposition separating the workers' camp from that of their exploiters, and it invited different populations to close ranks around "their" imperialism when faced with threats from that of another people. Was exploitation pleasant in one place on the pretext that somewhere else it took on more brutal forms and spared no pain? Did the revolutionary attitude not imply a discrediting of the capitalist world in general? Did communist theory not teach us that no one bourgeois government can be any worse than another, except in insignificant details, since the bourgeoisie itself defines itself as the regime of the worst [*le régime du pire*]?

No one would argue that Hitler and Mussolini were not dictators, but their liberal adversaries were hardly any better, given that there was not, and could not be, any such thing as bourgeois democracy. "At the very moment that a people gives itself representatives, it is no longer free; it ceases to be." Jean-Jacques Rousseau lived on: his critique of the representative system continued to inspire revolutionary thought in the 1930s. From this perspective, sovereignty is an inalienable good. To lend it, on any terms whatsoever, is to lose it. Representation destroys the body politic, although it tries to pass for its very incarnation. There is no delegation of power that is not an abdication on the part of those who transmit it and that is not a confiscation for the benefit of those who receive it. By entrusting its will to designated proxies, the sovereign group once constituted of the people reduces itself to impotence and kills off its organicity, only to be transformed into an inert mass incapable of governing itself. The people as an entity must be dissolved in order for the assembly to convene: the supposed instrument of democracy is merely the most subtle weapon of despotism. In short, there is no qualitative difference between the representative system and absolute government.

The thesis of the *Social Contract* is apparent in such thinking. It is true, nevertheless, that Rousseau must not be held responsible for the rigorism of his continuators. As Robert Dérathé recalls, "Toward the mid–eighteenth century, representative government as we think of it today, with assemblies elected by universal suffrage, did not exist in Europe, so to speak."[18] More often than not, parliaments were composed solely of an oligarchy jealous of its privileges, and it was only little by little, step by step, reform after reform, throughout the course of the nineteenth century, that representative government evolved toward democracy. But Rousseau's radical critique would outlive the conditions of its day and be invoked or taken up again for the purposes of condemning bourgeois regimes. With one slight difference, however: with his predilection for Greece, the author of the *Social Contract* constantly drew on ancient history for lessons that were suitable for instructing his readers. To denounce the modern idea of *representatives*, he took inspiration from Sparta and from cities where the people exercised their power by assembling on the town square: the year 1789 would do away with these references, and 1793 would substitute the *insurgent people* for the *assembled people* in antirepresentative argumentation. In the wake of Rousseau, who extolled the wisdom and serenity of ancient institutions, insurrectional effervescence would be exalted, and it was in the name of those tumultuous moments whose rare examples glisten in the firmament of history—*sans-culottisme*, the Commune, the Soviets of 1917, the Labor Councils in

Germany—that all other systems of government would be categorically condemned.

And then, of course, along came Marx to reinforce Rousseau. In saying that reality is disclosed on the level of the economy, in affirming the primacy of returns on production, he ascribed a necessity to this representative perversion that the first modern theorist merely described. The bourgeois political system *administers* the division between capital and labor. It has the twofold function of disguising class warfare as a fictitious equality and providing the ruling class with its instrument of domination. In contrast, true democracy would have to dissolve the political realm as a separate domain, and democracy would be "the achievement of a society that was immediate unto itself."[19] The end of politics: such was the utopia haunting the revolutionary mind-set, above and beyond its fantasies of a spontaneous movement or of the people rising up. The pro-worker agenda thus had two objectives: abolishing representation through direct democracy and abolishing politics itself with social transparency. And considered in light of this ideal, the various forms of power were just so many more or less efficient versions, so many more or less attractive faces of one and the same monotonous dictatorship of capital.

This doctrinaire purism was further strengthened by the nightmare of the recently ended world war. The "anti-antifascism" of the 1930s was a combination of the most theoretical abstraction and the very concrete terror of death in the trenches. Hitler? A double, a "remake," an exact copy of Kaiser Wilhelm. And in what it took to be a faltering moment of history, the extreme left seized the opportunity to redeem socialism. *This time* its members were determined not to succumb to the dubious spell of chauvinistic lyricism. The millions who had died in that war protected them from this temptation anyway. The sentimental idea of the fatherland had come out ruined by the slaughter at Verdun and in the Somme. Henceforth, faced with rising threats of war, the revolutionaries braced themselves with this one certainty: they would not forsake pacifism for patriotic delirium at the first clarion call. As redeemers of the Second International, they would have what it takes to give a radical, effective content to the watchword of defeatism. Stirred by both the desire for compensation and the trauma of recent carnage, the revolutionary minorities condemned antifascism with the unremitting vehemence of *those who would no longer be duped*. To stigmatize the preparation for war, pamphlets used the vocabulary of 1914: "Sacred union," "*Jusqu'au-boutisme*"— these cursed expressions masked the reality of Hitlerism. Their bewitching power got the better of the mounting bits of information and downplayed the inexorable originality of Nazi politics as nothing more than the same old imperialism.

We firmly state that we will no more march against Prussian militarism in 1935 than we did in 1914.[20]

Being internationalists, we will fight against chauvinistic propaganda, regardless of its source, as well as against the sacred union and any attempt to drag workers into a new imperialist war, be it on the pretext of so-called national defense that cannot exist in a capitalist regime or on the equally dishonest pretext of defending bourgeois democracies against fascism.[21]

The extreme left of the 1930s struggled against the shadows of its fathers and sought only one thing: to wash away the stain of nationalism, to purify itself of "*la victoire en chantant*" and other elucubrations of blind patriotism.[22] So absorbed was it in its desire to *do better* that it no longer had eyes for what was irreducible in the present. "The tradition of all the generations of dead weighs most heavily on the minds of the living." Imitation and the exact opposite tack were the two possible avatars of subjugation. Thus it was the oppressiveness described so well by Marx that gave rise to this critique of antifascism, one of the cornerstones of the *Munich spirit*.

But the dreaded war was not *a new 1914*. The scope of Nazi crimes exceeded even the most alarmist speculations. *Never again*! Such, in its uncompromising simplicity, was the sentiment engendered on the left by the memory of the Occupation combined with the discovery of the camps. Hitler put a face on Evil, and henceforth, all forms of oppression and violence would be compared to this model. As of the postwar period, the antifascism denounced as mystification became the least common denominator of leftist thought, the minimal position where democrats and revolutionaries met, the site where the usual distinction between politics and morality broke down.

   This unanimity explains the triumph of the *progressivist left* (that is, the left fascinated by the USSR) over all other possible forms of revolutionary thought. Russia pushed back the Nazi invader and contributed to the defeat of Hitler: the immensity of the willing sacrifice and the importance of the victory went a long way in erasing the misdeeds, deviations, or betrayals of Stalinism. As a result of the war, everything, or almost everything, could go back to the way it was before: the USSR recovered the lost aura of October 1917, and the European communist parties regained a leadership role. In the wake of the turmoil, and in the shock over the Nazi barbarity, it became possible again to identify the workers' *party*, the workers' *country*, and the working *class* as one and the same. And those who hesitated at this identification would soon be forced to surrender their distinctions to the logic of the cold war. As of 1947, "the horrible year," the Allied front suffered a definitive breakup serious enough to plunge the entire planet into the imminence of a third conflagration. This climate led to cut-and-dried positions. In a suddenly Manichaean world, abstention appeared to be no more possible than subtlety. The number two determined everything: a choice had to be made between the imperialist camp and that of socialism.

Where on the extreme left did anyone stand up against this blackmail? Not counting the vestigial sects that were petrified in their memories and that clung convulsively to the cult of their heroes—anarchists, Spartakists, *conseillistes*, Bordgists—the only living opposition to progressivism in France would crystallize around a small review: *Socialisme ou Barbarie* [Socialism or barbarity]. In the name of a strict logic of class, its founders, some former Trotskyites, contested the bloc logic that was in the process of taking hold. The key word of their discourse was autonomy of the proletariat—autonomy, which is to say, irreducibility or even hostility of the working class with respect to the official institutions of the workers' movement and the group of nations that claimed to have put it in power.

Russian society is not a socialist society, nor is it as degenerate a Workers' State as one would have it. It is a society of exploitation in which the proletariat, deprived of the fruits of its labor and the direction of its own activity, suffers the same fate it does under private capitalism.[23]

By promoting bureaucracy to the rank of ruling class, by radicalizing the Trots Kyites' timid, half-hearted critique of the fatherland of revolution, the intellectuals of *Socialisme ou Barbarie* revived the worker-power tradition interrupted by the war. Russia and America could very well hate each other, but the proletariat did not need to get into the quarrel since, in any case, the proletariat was the common object of their exploitation. The cold war forced the working class to choose which sauce—bourgeois or bureaucratic—capital would use to spice up its feast.

Thus the split was not effected between the two blocs but between "class" and the machinery of domination in all its forms. What a liberating displacement! Seeing their fellow Socialists crippled by uncertainties and exhausted by their swings of opinion, seeing how they vacillated between defending and condemning actual socialist practices, Castoriadis and Claude Lefort would conduct the first unsparing analysis of the Stalinist State. They would not ask themselves if the uprisings of Berlin, Poznan, or Budapest were instigated by the left or the right; they would not quibble over whether these really were workers' insurrections. But there was a high cost to pay for this exemplary lucidity. *Socialisme ou Barbarie*: its very title placed the review under the sign of the revolutionary apocalypse. Everything was decided in terms of all or nothing, antagonism of the purest form between capital and revolution. Capital—that is, a worldwide system of exploitation with bureaucracy as its ultimate form and bourgeois democracy its embryonic one ("no longer is bureaucracy a form of capitalism but rather, capitalism is a sort of bureaucracy").[24] Revolution—that is, a labor power that for the first time would not be exercised by delegation and would not be entrusted in any permanent way to its representatives, its State or its Party.[25] In its twofold simplicity, this mode of thought reduced the various systems of government to a single dictatorship and all manner of violence to exploitation. Socialism or barbarity: this alternative rendered impossible or inconceivable any organized barbarity that did not victimize the proletariat. What was there to say about a bourgeois regime more savage in its pursuit of an ethnic group posing no threat to it than it was against its natural enemy? Precisely this: nothing. Such cruelty, which of course was undeniable, was at the same time unthinkable within the logic of the workers' movement. What did come up for discussion and consideration were the hardship of capitalist slavery and the conflict of imperialist regimes. At the offices of *Socialisme ou Barbarie*, the traps and impasses of progressivism were all the more easily sidestepped in that antifascism failed to give rise to even the slightest echo. Four years *after* World War II, revolutionary thought took up where it had left off in the 1930s as if nothing had changed.

As the direct result of German, Italian, and Japanese production shutdowns within the excessively narrow confines of their respective markets, the war was only the first direct expression of the tendency toward a total concentration of production on the international scale, toward the regrouping of world capital around a single dominating pole. It was German capital that tried to play the unifying role by grouping European capital around itself. . . .

It was a question of benefiting the winning imperialism *through the annexation not only of underdeveloped countries but of capital itself in other imperialist countries in an attempt to organize the whole of the economy and of life around the world in view of the interests of a single, dominant imperialist group. The defeat of the Axis coalition gave the Allies an open playing field for world domination.*[26]

Written in 1949, this reflection establishes the absolute equivalence of the adversaries facing each other, makes them appear as quasi-interchangeable figures of bureaucracy, and assigns the same greedy rationale to each of them in periods of both war and peace. For the first time, there is evidence of the will to *humanize* Hitler—that is, to strip him of any baleful privilege and make him into a *representative of the inhumanity of capital like any other*.

In France, this worker-power sentiment remained confined to a small group of intellectuals. It was in Italy that a real mass movement emerged: *opéraïsme*, a labor movement in the 1960s (championed by *Potere Operaio*, named in honor of *Pouvoir ouvrier* [Worker Power], an outgrowth of *Socialisme ou Barbarie*) and, a decade later, autonomy, the inspiration of a few spin-offs that we have seen in France. This more widely accepted discourse also proved to be more aggressively reductive. Eradicate the tradition of popular Marxism and reconstruct a unilateral, bellicose workers' point of view on the social sphere; write contemporary history from the sole perspective of the antagonism that opposes capital with "the most offensive political force ever to have appeared in human society,"[27] namely the working class—this materialist reading neatly rids reality of those aspects of it that cannot be explained by the principle of class struggle. Hitlerism is then but one of many solutions to the problem plaguing capitalism in the interwar years: the control of labor-force movements. All that remains of the Nazi horror is the will to organize society as a society of producers, separated on different hierarchical levels. As for the war, it is the German command's response to the resistance to work, the moment of destruction of the working class, of its dragooning and its multinationalization through forced labor. Period.

These two interpretations of the last world conflict as a contest of different systems of imperialism or as the enslavement of the proletariat have one thing in common: they downplay the occurrence of the Jewish genocide. There is a reason to history—such is the fundamental certainty of all revolutionaries—and the genocide, a moment of madness, a sudden swerve off the path, does not fit within the framework of that reason. And so, discreetly, it is removed to the sidelines, or else it is reduced to that particularly brutal form of exploitation that treats workers as subhuman, as human flesh. In short, one chooses doctrinal fidelity over the complexity of things, and the Nazi phenomenon is divested of everything within it that is *opaque* to the logic of confrontation that is the supposed driving force of the world. This omission is carried out with a zeal more fervent for its being experienced as a battle on the revolutionary forefront: it is a matter of taking revolutionary theory out of the hands of the various authorities of the official workers' movement by interpreting the facts as this and only this: the actual, material existence of a real workers' autonomy.

THE PAST CONFORMED

Who made the big leap? Who went from omission to revision, from the scaling down of the genocide to the negation of the gas chambers? The most motivated, the most fanatical militants in the workers' movement. By suddenly depriving modern society of its principal foil, they believed that they were striking a mortal blow against it. It is the fantasy of the struggle, the devastating obsession with the fight, that feeds the undertaking to normalize the Nazi camps and turns the distortion of facts into heroism.

In contemporary political thought, fascism more than any other ideology plays the role of the devil. The Nazi universe constituted by the concentration camps is a most convenient hell. Antifascist ideology proposes the use of any and all means to save democracy in the face of fascism and dictatorships that are more or less comparable to it. But in fact this ideology is first and foremost a means of blurring the proletariat's own views with confusion and incorporating the working class into the effort to defend the capitalist world.[28]

Impeccable reasoning: Hitlerian anti-Semitism must be presented as a unique fact in history so that people will forget the countless sufferings produced by our society. There is thus nothing more *subversive* than the "revision" of Nazism: if the bourgeoisie's empty theory is exposed for what it is, then we, the mystified, will immediately awaken from our ideological sleep. There being no absolute horror to lessen or conceal the daily horror of our own sad lives, we will inevitably put an end to our concessions with the intolerable, and the final barrier holding us back from revolution will be lifted. According to this superb logic, the gas chambers function as a foil and are too essential to the consolidation of capitalism to have really existed. As long as the reality of this torture remains etched on the minds of the masses, workers go whistling off to the factory, content each day to have such good-hearted foremen, to be working shifts around the clock in so pleasant a world, and to take showers in what truly is hot and cold water. Let us imagine for a moment that the barbarity is declared fictitious, never to have occurred: the artificial paradise admits its infernal truth. Suddenly feeling the weight of their chains instead of remaining fascinated by the evil of the concentration camps, the workers say no to their exploitation and with a now unbridled, terrible, infallible and irremediable force, give themselves over to the abolition of the wage-earning class or, in other words, to the salvation of men.

Such supremely stupid "thinking" makes one want to laugh (or cry) with rage. The fact remains that it does not come out of the blue and that in order to pronounce liberal democracies equivalent to fascist dictatorships, its followers adopt the same tone and the same terminology that socialist parliamentarians used when justifying their politics of abstention on 20 January 1898. At that time, they denounced the Dreyfus affair as a "struggle between two rival groups of the bourgeoisie." Today's followers write: "the gas chambers are used to establish an unbridgeable gap between two opposing capitalist groups."[29]

And in both cases, one is witness to the same frenzied effort to *demystify*. The proletariat needs to be protected from all the diversions presented to it by those who would distract it from its mission. For although the proletariat is unhappy, although it is the ultimate incarnation of human sorrow, a strange constituent fragility makes it forget its suffering at the slightest distraction. "All the unhappiness of men," said Pascal, "comes from a single source, which is not knowing how to remain still in a room." All the misfortunes of the revolution, say his modern apostles, result from the very vain agitation of men. Capricious even in their oppression, they get riled up and fool themselves with futile passions or imaginary objects of longing. It is on account of this inconstancy that the old mole is growing older and the dialectic is stalled.

To put this in anecdotal terms, an individual's whim took on the proportions of a public affair on the day in 1978 that Pierre Guillaume decided to back Faurisson and mobilize his little militant team on the professor's behalf. Guillaume began his political career at *Socialisme ou Barbarie*. The group dissolved in the late 1960s, split as it was between those who were weary of rehashing historical materialism and wanted to expand their thinking on the social question and those who were the traditionalists of revolution. Together with other members of the latter persuasion, Pierre Guillaume participated in founding a bookstore, La Vieille Taupe [the Old Mole], which exhumed, exposed, and celebrated everything the official workers' movement had suppressed, emphasizing in particular the great maligned prophets of intransigence: Anton Pannekoek, Karl Korsch, Herman Gorter, Otto Ruhle, and especially the spiritual father of the Italian communist left, Amedeo Bordiga, who devoted all his theoretical energy to assailing the "illusion of democracy" and denouncing antifascism as the worst of all the monstrosities produced by fascism. As early as 1953, subscribers of *Socialisme ou Barbarie* could read in the doctrines of Italy's internationalist communist party (Bordiga's sect): "Antifascism is only the most recent ideological and political lie behind which capitalism played the card of its own class-preservation during World War II."[30] For such hard-line discourse, which La Vieille Taupe adopted and cultivated, the genocide of the Jews was one event too many, a thorn in the rose of proletarian Reason because it had created an unbridgeable chasm between fascist and democrat. Then along came an obscure, solitary professor from Lyons who tried to remove the thorn. Having accumulated "two hundred kilograms of work documents representing the careful examination of several tons of texts," he proved the impossible monstrosity never in fact took place, and thus he erased from history that incongruity, that challenge to the very logic of the class struggle: the gas chambers of the Nazi camps.[31] To discover a direction in the evolving course of things is also, surreptitiously, to prevent it from following another itinerary. "Revisionism" is the moment in which this theoretical maxim becomes applicable. That which has no intelligible status is finally cast with empirical nonexistence: from then on, no obstacle impedes the majestic reconciliation of the real with the rational.

Doubly commendable, Faurisson transformed an improbable event into a *nonevent* and furnished purely deductive thinking with the alibi of empiricism, of induction. Thanks to him, simple workers' prejudice took on the scientific appearance of investigation. It is easy to see why the unemployed militants of La Vieille Taupe were immediately so taken with Faurisson and the weight of his briefcase.[32] These metaphysicians, these "logico-communists," had an unhealthy respect for the sheer mass of the reputed documentation ("two hundred kilograms," "several tons of texts") that reduced their *a priori* to minutia, transfigured these militants themselves into researchers, and turned their contempt for the real into a passion for detail.

It hardly matters what the professor's own motivations might have been. The telling fact is that a few purists of the revolution pulled him out of the desperate isolation into which he seemed to be falling irretrievably. And needless to say, these militants participate in the falsification with a good faith that is above and beyond suspicion. No task is too daunting for them when it comes to conforming the face of history to the unflinchingly restrictive idea they make of it. They *know* that the gas chambers are a myth in the same way that Wilhelm Liebknecht knew that Dreyfus was guilty. Auschwitz serves their enemy's purpose, hence their fervor to contest the evidence of its reality by every means possible, including the most fraudulent. For the evidence of genocide is just so many deceptions, so many traps laid for anticapitalist radicality, designed to force it into dishonest compromise and eventual loss of resolve.

The militant revolutionaries supporting Faurisson applaud themselves over and over again for defending a thesis so contrary to their longest-held convictions. From this they gain the glorious, intoxicating impression that they are thinking *in opposition to themselves*. And from this disinterestedness, they draw still more proof of having gained access to what is true. "We say the gas chambers are a lie. Now we cannot be suspected of harboring the slightest weakness for Hitler's imperialism (we who, without hesitation, would have chosen to side with the Resistance). We do not share the *ideology* of our discovery. Is that simple fact not the best guarantee of its validity? Does our striving to be impartial not confirm the soundness of our thesis?" And if one uncovers a fascist temptation in their discourse, if one charges them with intentions that they never had, "those who put the dead back on their feet"[33] become reinvigorated by this slander and see within it the flattering image of martyrs of truth, thereby assuring themselves that they are the victims of a plot to stifle history.

Let us therefore cease to favor these anticapitalists with the reproach they need in order to feel persecuted. Such an affront is a gift: it fortifies their vanity, it ennobles their itinerary, by making them believe that *in spite of themselves* they are bowing to the power of facts when they are really just bending history to their conception of the world. What defines them is their ardent desire to restore to communism its cutting edge, now dull from a half-century of caricature, and to shield the purity of the rupture with bourgeois domination from all dishonest compromise. Is this discourse monstrous? No doubt, but monstrous does not mean without ties. There are some extravagant behaviors that are nothing more than excesses of orthodoxy. The revisionist left unites around the Marxist monument, that masterpiece in peril. These sons proclaim the supremacy of the father with an impatience all the more scandalized because his other children are abandoning him. The more "de-Marxized" modern thought becomes, the more urgent and necessary a return to Marx appears to them. In truth, if they are trying to rehabilitate someone, it is Marx, not Hitler—Marx disfigured by all the regimes that claim him as their inspiration, Marx abhorred by the impatient, by the deserters who throw out the baby with the bathwater and think that in a single reprimand they can confound the doctrine with its pseudo-applications. Their dreams are filled with visions of the apocalypse, not of pagan feasts in the German forests or neo-Nazi parades. Global revolution, total salvation, radical change—these *fundamentalists* declare their allegiance to the principle of all or nothing and go off to war against the reformists who have watered it down or against the bureaucrats who borrow its rhetoric to justify their own despotism. Everyone else has obscured, tampered with, or toned down the message.

Only they, the fundamentalists, are preserving its rigor. Only they are fighting "those who in every time and place revise, update, renovate or innovate"; only they snatch away the mask of good-naturedness donned by democracies, ridicule the "grand ineptitude of the new rhetorics," and know how to pinpoint the invariance of the Theory amidst the joltings and anarchy of history.[34]

One must therefore forego the habit of treating the shock troops of "revisionism" as blond brutes: there is no sadism driving them, no love of the swastika, no nostalgia for the totalitarian right. Their only concern is to take up position *to the left of all lefts*: an abstract realm, an absolute meta-language, an impregnable fortress from which to condemn half-heartedness and dishonest compromise without being subject to any judgment themselves. Accused of sympathy for the horror of the camps, they conceive of themselves, amidst traitors and dupes, as the ultimate champions of the revolutionary idea: winners by knockout in the escalating competition among the small groups vying to make the principle of radicality their own.

A QUESTION OF PRIORITY

What seems obvious is not really the case: it is not hatred against the Jews that leads to clearing Hitler of his attempt at genocide; it is abstract love for the working class. The proletariat is thoroughly invincible only because it is absolutely subservient, and it is the very idea of humanity incarnate only because "humanity alone, infinite in its distress and its rights" subsists within it.[35] Workers are the target of a generic injustice: no class, no nation, or ethnic group must be allowed to rob them of their title. The negators of the gas chambers do not reproach the Jews for being Jews (that is to say, different, monotheistic, obscurantist, or greedy) but for muddling up the movement of history, *for violating the dialectic*, by claiming for themselves a prejudice even worse than the wrong to which the working class is subjected daily. Modern history claims that each day a crime is committed against the labor force. It is up to the revolutionaries to keep reminding people of just how outrageous this scandal is and to prevent society from overlooking it by focusing attention on lesser crimes. Those who today consider antifascism to be a myth and the story of the genocide a trompe l'oeil are no more Judeophobic than were the Socialists at the time of the Dreyfus affair. They simply cannot tolerate a minor player who thinks he can change things around and assume the leading role.

The Social Revolution was prepared in accordance with familiar rules; the magic words of class struggle and conquest of public powers pronounced at just the right moment would provide the means to revolutionize the world without destroying peoples' souls. . . . and then there you have this captain, one of the bourgeoisie, who is ill-advised enough to stir up an affair, and not a fitting affair that can be of benefit elsewhere and which coincides with the prophets' predictions but an affair like no other in the entire history of the world. The prophets dislike reality when it exceeds all prophecy.[36]

Of what are the Jews guilty? Of Auschwitz—which is to say, of an inconvenient, unclassifiable massacre the likes of which the prophets could not foresee, one that remains an outrage to revolutionary theory. With the negation, the Jews simply are punished for not staying in their place and for constantly overstepping the bounds of the category to which the dialectic of history, in all its omniscience, has assigned them: the category of scapegoat. Socialist ideology combats anti-Semitism by reducing it to a technique of governing: the practical means of deflecting popular disarray, the causes of which must be concealed at all costs, onto a vulnerable, marginalized group. Those who are truly to blame for it shield themselves behind the falsely accused, and the public as a whole regains a phony homogeneity instead of pursuing to its breaking point the division plaguing society. From this perspective the Jews are a *godsend* for capitalism. The exploited would find violence irresistible if these pariahs did not dissipate it by polarizing it on themselves. Designated as the troublemakers causing all the problems, they provide the public with the illusion of having regained control over its destiny, and they allow for the reconciliation of the oppressors with the slaves. Conclusion: the ruling classes need the scapegoat Jew for their own survival. Firmly convinced of this, Franz Neumann (one of the theorists of the Frankfurt School) could write, in 1942: "The internal political value of anti-Semitism will never allow a complete extermination of the Jews."[37]

No one admires capitalism more than its mortal enemies, and the current revision of the genocide feeds on this adulation. There is too great a respect for the bourgeoisie to believe it capable of getting worked up enough to satisfy a murderous passion at the expense of its own needs. One would seriously underestimate the bourgeoisie if one were to think that even for a moment it could cease to be functional and neglect its class interest or the icy waters of utilitarian reason just to satisfy a savage impulse. That an expiatory victim should be promoted to the rank of absolute enemy, that it should be necessary to take literally Goering's statement "This is not the second world war, this is the War of the Races": such is the impropriety, the theoretical scandal that the first champions of Faurisson felt he had rightly disproved.

And so now the Nazis slip on the discarded mantle of the whipping boy. Is society not rebuilding its unity on supposed Nazi crimes, just as in former times it was quasi-unanimous in denouncing the occult power of Israel?

In the German capitalist system shaken by World War I, anti-Semitism cynically served to bring political unity to heterogeneous social strata and to make them loyal to the State. Antifascism has the same political function and uses the same psychological mechanisms, even though the target is different. We must be done with anti-Semitism. We must be done with antifascism. Both are socialism for idiots.[38]

This rigorously *materialist* thinking produces a monstrous amalgam unlike any that the most imaginative Judeophobe could ever have dreamed up: the Jew and the Nazi are variants of one and the same function, the avatars of that substitutive victim who attracts and traps working-class violence. The will to defend the proletariat's seat of honor thus culminates in the negation of the genocide and the pure and simple assimilation of the torturer and the tortured.

2

War Logic and *Langue de bois*

Free up the forces of hatred indispensable to the edification of the new world. Since power lies at the tip of a gun, take pedagogical care to aim the proletarians' weapon at its true target. Educate their resentment, rechannel their violence instead of letting it go to waste on Hitler, that old punching bag, that cardboard cutout from the shooting gallery. Such is the objective of the abstract consciences for whom fascism is only a somewhat more savage episode of capitalism, a scarcely amplified expression of planetary barbarity. As for their method, it is ruthless. The negators of the genocide unceremoniously subordinate history as it was lived to history as it is conceived; they tighten the screws until finally there no longer exists the slightest interplay between an event and the concept under which it is to be classified. They look to that docile oracle, the past, to ratify their knowledge, fortify their activism, and announce the apocalypse here and now. They believe themselves to be the ultimate, courageous guardians of the true sense of things. And Nazi passion, which resists assimilation into their construct and remains dangerously outside it, *plays hooky from history* so to speak: it is an intolerable disturbance with which they refuse to make even the slightest compromise. Filled with aversion for the opportunists who adapt the theory to the real, they eliminate from the real any and all elements that contest the truth of the theory. These revolutionaries are swimming against the tide of their contemporaries: while so many others are changing under the influence of the current fashion or in the grip of disillusionment, these revolutionaries prefer the revision of history to that of their beliefs. The very reason for their involvement in this new battle is to salvage the principles of "all or nothing" and the final struggle, standards that went by the wayside as militant thought and practice ebbed. Still in the sway of the bittersweet joys of sectarianism, they seem a bit like the last of the Mohicans.

Hitler is whitewashed, his crimes are rationalized, and the fierceness of his violence is whittled down to regular proportions—and all these efforts to normalize him are aimed at saving the principle of revolution! The thought is ridiculous, the steps taken extravagant. Are they crazy? Are they wicked? Are they anachronistic? All of the above, no doubt, and yet not one of these qualities allows us to set the "revisionists" apart from common humanity. The age in which we are living cannot be considered free and clear of their ravings. It would be a mistake to abandon ourselves to indignation, to condescension, or to psychoanalyzing these pious militants, to shutting them off in their prehistory or their delirium on the pretext that they are speaking a dead tongue with an imperturbable sense of self-importance as if it were the only *living* language. In so doing, we would be neglecting the essential, namely the fact that for the benefit of their archaic enterprise, these "revisionists" are making use of one of modernity's ordinary behaviors: the scrambling of information through interpretation, the denial of fact turned into the exegesis of discourse, the *refusal to know* what is said sublimated in the will to know *more* about the person speaking.

KRAVCHENKO

Another trial concerning concentration camps. But these camps were Soviet ones, and in 1949, casting the slightest shadow on the Stalingrad sun was tantamount to siding with the reactionary bloc. Victor Kravchenko committed just this blasphemy in the book he published three years after he asked for political asylum in the United States. Scarcely had the work been translated when *Les Lettres françaises*, a communist weekly that had grown out of the Resistance, ran an article under the unambiguous headline "How Kravchenko was Fabricated." Believing he had been slandered, the author of the book filed suit against the writer of the article and the director of the publication, and from 24 January to 6 April 1949, the court at the Palais de Justice of Paris was the stage of a fascinating confrontation. On the one side were the victims of Stalinist repression, survivors of the camps who came to tell of their experience and corroborate Kravchenko's work. On the other was a who's who of French progressivism, eminent members of the Communist Party and like-minded activists, every last element of the left stepping forth to purify the USSR of the accusations that were sullying it. Confrontation? The word "contiguity" would be more fitting to describe the arrogance with which French Stalinists impugned the bothersome witnesses and froze the October Revolution in its inalterable perfection. These Faurissonians of the Gulag remained impervious to the wealth of evidence and the bluntness of the testimony. Nothing could touch them, not even the painful testimony of Margarete Buber-Neumann, turned over to the Nazis in the wake of the German-Soviet nonaggression pact and finishing out at Ravensbrück a concentration camp stint that began in the Siberian steppe. How did they manage not *to take it in* and to keep their idea of Bolshevism separate from the actual experience of its victims? They did as the "revisionists" do: they deciphered, divulged, unveiled: they put all of their energy into a veritable interpretative orgy. Who was speaking? Why? For what purpose? What was Kravchenko's strategy in organizing this circus of a trial? Who was behind him? Who was pulling the strings? What were the secret motives behind the operation? Faced with the accumulation of evidence, the Stalinists resorted to two opposite readings that were also two variants of the same effort to defuse allegations. Either they treated the text as a closed entity and subjected it to the ruthless scrutiny of the literary critic: "I believe that through the internal investigation of this book, it is possible to show the mechanics of its fabrication," affirmed the witness Roger Garaudy, who concluded upon investigation: "Herein we have established the dictionary of clichés of anti-Sovietism, and this frail structure is readily apparent by the end of the book."[1] Or else they uncovered and explored the essential connection in discourse between the speaker and that about which he was speaking: the account of an experience became the account of oneself, and no longer displayed actions but a set of signs and symptoms to be deciphered. The referent was put to death twice over: first, through the accession of testimony to the rank of (bad) literature; and second, through the transformation of the report into *confession*, an invisible semiological coup d'état that dismissed the realistic function of the message for the sole benefit of its expressive one. Hence the unbearable arrogance of the listener. He was no longer a receiver but a sovereign. By going back from text to author, and from author to context, it was he and he alone who held in his possession the truth of opposing claims: "I believe that this book is untrue, and doubly so, and that Mr. Kravchenko did not choose freedom because under the conditions in which he found himself in the United States, his circumstances were those of a renegade. He could not have chosen, because a renegade is not free to choose, because when you are the renegade of a cause, you inevitably become the agent or the servant of the cause you just abandoned, despite whatever justification you might have or think you have."[2]

Master Pathelin played the fool so as not to understand.[3] With the same goal in mind, Master Militant adopted the opposite behavior: he played the role of the intellectually superior. Instead of rejecting the testimony, pretending that he failed to understand it, he understood it *better* and deciphered the hidden confession or the propaganda effort behind its misleading realism. Far from closing his eyes, he made a thorough examination and replaced the tactic of imbecility with that of deciphering. Leaving behind the real as he turned to hermeneutics, he saw his blindness as a surplus of lucidity (it was a matter of seeing beyond appearances) and his deafness as a more acute perception of the connotations and insinuations that were the shadowy truth of the Other, the texture of his word.

Just look at what happened to David Rousset. As soon as he published an appeal to former deportees to Nazi camps so that they might investigate the Soviet concentration camp world, he was discredited on the basis of his motivations (war), his sources (imperialism), and his support (*Le Figaro littéraire*). "Rousset provided some facts, and published a no doubt highly accurate map of the Gulag, but its discernible American origin was enough to make it seem bogus to me."[4]

In terms of method, the negators of the gas chambers are the spiritual sons of the great Stalinists. With the same critical fervor, they disqualify annoying testimony on the basis of its secret intent. Was it not in the interest of the Georgian egocrat and bourgeois democracies to condemn their vanquished adversary, to paint his guilt with the darkest colors, and to inflate Nazi horror to paroxysmal proportion? Were the gas chambers not the unheard of and thus *providential* atrocity that would forever prevent any and all rapprochement between the victors and their enemies? It is the irony of history that in order to hate the generalissimo more thoroughly, those who would revise the genocide are adopting for their own use the very same tactics used by the Party's artillerymen during the cold war. It is among its fiercest adversaries that Stalinism finds its most like-minded disciples. For not every aspect of what was known as the Stalinist phenomenon died with the Twentieth Congress, the Kruschev report, or even the declared anti-Stalinism of leftist thought. What disappeared was the pomposity, the turgidity, the bombast, the whole teeming, hysterical bestiary that, at the least criticism, at the slightest reticence, labeled you a viper, a typing hyena, a slimy rat, or a jackal. It is true that the verbal outrageousness and the absolutely insane violence of these accusations continue to astound us. It is a wild and crazy vocabulary that today's most ardent extremist would have qualms about using. But we should not conclude that this disuse signals the replacement of absolute fury with complete awareness. It is within the *langue de bois* itself—the rigid, stereotypical language of ideological platitudes—that composure has succeeded hysteria.[5] A position that blocks out the real goes quite well with a toned-down lexicon of seeming moderation. Contrary to what ugly Stalinist folklore would have us believe, it is not vehemence or lyrical rage that is essential to the sociopolitical mechanism but rather the unrelenting practice of interpretation.

And one risks not seeing the true nature of this method if one describes it in religious terms, a common practice nowadays. Were they protecting their little corner of utopia, those members of the left who took turns on the witness stand in order to revile Kravchenko or denounce Rousset's infamous maneuvers? Was it the pressing need for a terrestrial paradise, for a golden age somewhere here on earth, that pushed them to treat all revelations about Stalinist reality as schemes or calumny? Perhaps. But it was not from *faith* itself that these zealots gained their self-importance. It was from the dizzying certainty of having once and for all abolished idols and revealed the essence of religions. They *believed they no longer believed*: this conviction made their discourse invulnerable. They had gotten beyond appearances and attained that sublime height, that position of infallibility engendered not by belief but by the radical critique of all forms of devotion. Confident in their knowledge, they could look back down on the world euphorically, for they "knew" that religion, in the usual sense of the term, was the liturgical variant of a single, unique lullaby: that famous bourgeois ideology that soothed the masses to sleep in the illusion of living in *a society with no history*. The Individual, Nature, Christ, the Soul: so many divinities offered up for adoration by the masses in order to hide the material principle of historicity—the class struggle. In short the progressivists had not found God in Lenin; they had discovered the *struggle* at the very base of all reality. "The king is naked," they proudly thought; "historical materialism has stripped him of all his ornaments, of all his *pious* lies." To believe or to have others believe it possible that a sector of activity, that any one of life's domains, however modest or personal it might be, could be shielded from the implacable law of the antagonism between labor and capital: such was the supreme mystification, such was piety and religious regression. No manner of speech could boast that it was neutral: history had two poles; the world was divided into two camps. And the rest was deception and camouflage. Henceforth, did clear-sightedness not require eluding the snares of ideology and probing all discourse so as to disclose their strategy and uncover their source? This fanaticism was not religious but materialist, for it squared off against its contradictors with a world devoid of illusion, and this world necessarily entailed the practice of inquisition.

More profoundly, the relationship between war and religion was reversed with the irruption of the great secular ideologies. In former times people had their religious faith, and they went to war to defend it or to propagate it abroad. In our secularized world, the postulate of universal struggle transforms the most reasonable people into visionaries. We have gone from the soldier monk to the monk soldier, so to speak; and ever since this shift occurred (in our climes, at least), religious principle has ceased to engender military behaviors, but military principle (combat as the *driving force* of history) exalts its followers, produces and reproduces continuously the uncompromising faith and blind zeal that are the basis of religious fanaticism.

Perhaps not enough attention has been paid to the surreptitious or unconscious charms inherent in the concept of the struggle. The social war, history's hidden god, places its participants under the perpetual, delightful obligation of unmasking the adversary. Now, to unmask is to hold oneself up as the Master of Truth, to know more about the Other than what he says and what he knows himself, and to pair his discourse with a deeper one that decodes it and brings its true meaning to light. Such unveiling is one marvelous power: through it, and for all of eternity, I am in possession of what comes to me from without; I decipher before I understand, or at least I listen to a message only to know whom it serves and whence it comes.

In order to lay the groundwork for a new war intended to destroy the Soviet Union, the Kravchenko trial in Paris has been blown out of proportion. This trial will unmask the warmongers, exposing the true character of the slimy rat appearing before the Paris court, and it will unveil the roaring, bestial mouths of the protectors of this miserable traitor.[6]

War logic gives rise to a language that is tight, closed, protected against any disturbance, and permanently removed from the rigors of existence: one need only retranslate the surprises or denials of reality into terms of a military offensive to wind up immediately back on *familiar ground*. In a world inhabited by combatants, "others" can adopt one of only two possible appearances: the other will be either an Adversary or a Devotee, and this alternative deprives him of his strangeness in advance. Should he nevertheless force his way into the fortress or bunker that the self has become under the influence of the idea of the struggle, there remains an ultimate means of neutralizing him and putting him back in his place: asking oneself from whence he speaks. This magical question dissipates momentary trouble by evacuating the intruder: summoned to reintegrate his camp, he is cataloged all over again, pinned to an image that a brief oversight had allowed him to escape. There is no one more deaf at times than he who refuses to let himself be deluded: by listening only to the ulterior motive or the underlying intention, he can forget about what is obvious in the message, sidestep the discourse through recourse to the unspoken, and discount the alterity of his interlocutor as opposition to his interests. He has designated the enemy. The gap is sealed, and his convictions, which were momentarily shaken, are once again intact. Paradoxically the idea of war promises a risk-free exchange with exterior reality.

Situate truth in the struggle, and without even realizing it, you acquire an absolutely peremptory political consciousness; history conceived as conflict neutralizes confrontation with exteriority and wards off the threat posed to any intellectual system by the random, unspecified aspects of events. The armor is solid; penetration is impossible: no longer is there a single chink through which something new could enter the mind.

Seek to engage the fight in the semblance of chaos: nothing stands up to that great binary split; everything goes back to the established antagonism. The toughest circumstances, the most unforeseen outburst, the most irreverent or overwhelming testimony return *calmly and quietly* to their places in this *raging* war. The orderliness of the conflict governs the totality of the real; the unthinkable itself is absorbed in the known, in the already-thought. And it is in this way that irrefutable *proof* of how the camps worked, and of their vocation to exterminate, could be turned around into the *sign* of a conspiracy—against the USSR, in the case of the Gulag, and in favor of the reinforcement of imperialism, of Soviet bureaucracy, or of the State of Israel, in the case of the Nazi massacres.

DEMYSTIFICATION OF THE IMAGE

With the current crisis in ideologies, we think of ourselves as being immune to dogmatism. And it would even be tempting to see within "revisionism" the agony, the *delirium tremens* of an ideology on the verge of death. In the days of the Stalinists, military psychosis was widespread as the cold war weighed heavily on everyone's mind. The negators of the genocide, on the other hand, are ridiculous, mentally unbalanced fighters who believe they are dealing the deathblow to capitalism while no one even notices their fury. It would be wrong, however, to jump to the hasty conclusion that this is cause for celebration. We are living in an uncertain time when the thaw coincides with freezing on another front. Whereas the *langue de bois* seems to be dying of neglect, the critique of mass media is taking war logic to new heights.

Do not believe in images, pay less attention to the news itself than to the media broadcasting it, force yourself away from the innocent confusion of the real and the sign, break the spell of the spectacle, apply to the letter these great principles of vigilance, and you are sure never to be disturbed by the sudden appearance of the unforeseen. The concept of the society of spectacle initiates the "disarticulation of the real into successive, equivalent signs":[7] the very materiality of facts disappears in the universality of images. The world is no longer reflected but consumed by false appearances, and all that is left of an event is the daily lie our oppressors invite us to believe. An action that becomes *news* is more or less "vaporized," dissolved in the very information that disseminates it, and the information itself is reduced to being its own support. No longer is there anything *real*—just a *medium* in the hands of a *power*. "The spectacle is the existing order's uninterrupted discourse about itself, its laudatory monologue. It is the self-portrait of power in the epoch of its totalitarian management of the conditions of existence."[8]

In replacing the naïve notion of the image-as-reflection with the intelligent one of the image-as-spectacle, one endows oneself with a quasi-supernatural faculty, that of refusing all information coming from the outside that cannot be digested. Using the *critical* alibi of resisting the subterfuges of representation, one can eliminate the intruder, namely the thing represented. Thus at a time when technology is offering the quasi-simultaneous reproduction of what is happening in the world, one is witnessing a strategy of perfect isolation being developed under the cover of suspicion and in the conspicuous presence of war.

"Wouldn't it be simpler for the government to dissolve the people and elect a new one?" asked Brecht after the labor revolt of East Berlin in 1953. Demystification of the image gives to each private citizen what the exercise of power denies even the most totalitarian state: the possibility of correcting current events as they unfold by "derealizing" those events that are troublesome or irritating. The radical critique of the media ensures one's vision of the world against the devastating assaults by the principle of reality. Well ensconced in one's defiance, a peaceful inhabitant of suspicion, one can always counteract disconcerting images with a blunt refusal—and all in the name of the *interests* motivating their distribution and the political *maneuvers* being hatched in the shadow of the spectacle.

As we recall, the victory of the Khmer Rouge was met with unbridled joy by the vast majority of those on the left. In Cambodia as in Vietnam, Uncle Sam was being put to rout, the people were heroically freeing themselves from his horrifying grip, and the deplorable, corrupt puppet regime set up by the premier world power was about to bow to the revolutionary will of a peasant army.

Almost immediately, however, disturbing rumors concerning democratic Kampuchea began to circulate: with Phnom Penh barely in hand, its liberators were turning its entire population out to the paddy field; then, from the mouths of the first refugees came word that the subjects of the new regime were being forced to perform ten hours of farm labor or terracing work per day "on a diet reduced to two bowls of rice and thin soup,"[9] that children were being assigned to the production of goods as of the age of twelve or even eight in certain sectors; that the "class enemy" (a broad category encompassing most intellectuals, religious figures, and anyone who made it his business to know a foreign language) was being unmercifully hunted down, tortured, and killed.

It is true that this news remained fragmentary and uncertain because the Khmer Rouge regime had completely shut itself off from the outside world. No foreign journalists were authorized to enter the country. A significant portion of the Western left was able to maintain *confidence* in and sympathy for the Cambodian experience precisely because of this *censorship*—that is, because information was lacking, the decision by Pol Pot and his men to screen the country from the imperialist gaze seemed like evidence of both clear-sightedness and radicality. Their refusal to let cameras into Cambodia revealed a hatred for the West that in Third World thinking is the greatest proof of authenticity a burgeoning revolution can offer. And then, too, was this ravaged country not justified in undertaking its reconstruction without having its oppressors in the way? Was it not right to guard against the brainwashing and propaganda campaigns that the American press, or presses with allegiance to America, would surely wage, if Kampuchea opened up enough to invite journalists in?

The first reports nevertheless appeared, in particular the film made in 1978 by the Yugoslavian journalist Nicolas Victorovic. These terrible images revealed the dictatorship's exploits: ghost towns, closed universities, colonies of children performing hard labor, the entire country transformed into one huge work camp. With the Vietnam invasion, the silence that had been weighing down on Kampuchea for several long years was broken once and for all: the Western media were finally reporting the unique crime that those in charge of the revolution had committed against their own people.[10] Was it fitting to speak of planned extermination or to go so far as to forge the novel concept of "autogenocide"? In any case it certainly seemed that in passing from rumor to image, the atrocity was undeniable. But that was without taking into account the sort of *veneration* or *paranoid love* that the worst detractors of the "System" felt toward it. The harder one fights against imperialism, the more one bows to its Machiavellian intelligence. If the West was flaunting its pity for the Cambodian people, if it was making a show of the turpitude of Cambodia's leaders and describing the toppled regime as "one of the most oppressive powers known to history,"[11] you could be sure that such bombastic emotion stemmed from cold calculation, that there were cruel reasons behind this sudden display of humanitarian sentiment.

A few of the big names in the anti-imperialist struggle thus took it upon themselves to "interrogate" the images—that is, to stand up to alienation and ask the impertinent question "What is it hiding?" instead of taking in the parade of visual signs like some stupid, passive couch potato. And it was in this way that the West's *delayed* interest in Cambodia was recoded as a symptomatic *rush*: imperialism excused its own wrongdoings—the crimes it had just committed (the war in Vietnam) and those it was in the process of supporting (the Timor massacres)—by using the Pol Pot model of socialism as both a screen and a foil.

It is obvious that there exists a Western delirium that seems to be the flip side of a great rationality and that there is a Western bias that seems to be the flip side of a great efficiency. Obvious as long as one takes into account that the West is at war. *And that it is waging its war through peaceful means which are characteristic of a cultural war: "If you want war, pretend you are making peace." The West's principal weapon is its monopoly on information (and disinformation) along with the financial establishment of multinational corporations. It is winning the war of words and images. . . . The best source of propaganda for the West was the Pol Pot regime. We needed that ogre, that foil.*

So said Régis Debray in a memorable roundtable discussion with Noam Chomsky published under the title "Narration and Power" by the review *Change*.[12] And this mode of thinking became familiar to us as of the beginning of this work: we are already accustomed to police action that searches beneath a proclaimed injustice to find the true misdeed hidden by the exhibition. We have already seen how this scapegoat logic turns modern dictatorships into the West's sacrificial victims. But in this conversation between

Chomsky and Debray, the argumentation moved up a notch: the American linguist figured the number of victims of Khmer Rouge repression to be one hundred thousand. "And," he added, "we should probably take into account local reprisals by peasants."[13] In other words the Cambodian regime was probably not exactly heaven on earth, but it was in vain that its leaders said, "The revolution needs only a million and a half to two million Cambodians to build the country." They were innocent of the principal crime of which they were accused, that of having reduced their people to slavery, having let the unfit die, and having annihilated everyone who on the basis of culture or parentage was denied access into the kingdom of the New Man. And if they were innocent, it was precisely because the media judged them to be guilty. The *absence* of genocide was attested to by its *presence* in the images from the news.

THE HOLOCAUST EFFECT

If history reveals itself in the concept of the struggle, if war affects the mind like the very truth of the real, then as we have seen, there no longer can be any such thing as chance. Every apparent coincidence and all random reality merely translate an insufficiency or a naïveté of reflection. The required itinerary for lucidity leads from the surface downwards, from the arbitrary fact to the underground will that inhabits it. In its unpolished, elementary version, this will is defined as a *plot*. It is a satanic (or redemptive) design, a plan of domination (or enfranchisement) consciously if not coldly premeditated by its agents. In its sophisticated (that is to say, nonsubjective) version, this will is a force that directs its subjects without their knowing it, an order or a structure placed above people and from which they are powerless to escape. Historical materialism or the plot theory: revolutionary consciousness is always oscillating between these two poles. When cooler heads prevail, there is talk of capital or imperialism, abstract entities, totalities that transcend individuals, encompass them, and determine their actions. When temperatures rise, in the heat of confrontation, revolutionary impatience *prefers faces to structures*: there is a shift from capital to bosses, or even to the two hundred families,[14] from imperialism to meetings behind closed doors, to the clandestine colorfulness of multinational establishments, the Pentagon, or the Tricontinental. But the morphology of the Adversary is of little importance; political realism prescribes first and foremost that one know how to evaluate his strength. Withholding the least circumstance from the rigor of confrontation would amount to insulting him and to taking the deadly risk of underestimating him. Nothing is fortuitous: such is the fundamental principle of war logic.

But a new weapon has been born, one that changes the stakes and the conditions of battle. This weapon is the spectacle. In this audiovisual era, signs have taken hold of the world. Henceforth the true militant question is no longer "Who stands to gain from this crime?" but "Who stands to gain from this image?" And the focus of suspicion shifts, and the question becomes more radical: war logic no longer questions the origin but rather the reality of the event at issue. It was obviously in the interest of imperialist countries to present the world with a genocide in Cambodia. One can therefore conclude that indeed mistakes were made, and exactions and even atrocities occurred, but there was no genocide. Likewise "our" revisionists contend that Western viewers in general were moved by the movie *Holocaust*. This organized trauma, this unanimous emotionalism, must therefore cast doubt on the scope if not the reality of the extermination suffered by the Jews. The obsession with the struggle reduced every event to a subjective intention or a strategy. In the framework of the war of images, power is not content to make history: it manipulates it. The issue is no longer one of merely denouncing its actions; its deceptions and lies must be undone as well. The denial of an event thereby achieves its own industrial revolution. Following the already considerable paranoid virtualities of a police vision of history, along comes a technique of revision whose possibilities are infinite. The refusal to believe in the existence of the gas chambers is only one particular example of this new brand of revisionism.[15]

To put it another way, we are experiencing today the Holocaust effect. All the criticism that the movie made for American television deserves has already been leveled against it. An insipidly sentimental version of the genocide, this miniseries gives only a lame idea of the war against the Jews, with the possible exception of the episode concerning the growing danger of war. Well short of faithfully depicting disaster, it replaces concrete horror with clichés of horror; it brings the unimaginable back to the realm of the déjà vu of melodrama, to the tried-and-true recipes of flashy catastrophes. That moment in history is ruthlessly standardized by the universal idiom of mass culture. No doubt the viewer is moved to tears, but it is in the same way as with *Gone with the Wind*, or even *A Man and a Woman*. The same effects produce the same sobs. With *Holocaust*, insipidness takes over a formerly irreducible domain and further augments the range of its domination. Such is the tyranny of pathos that submits *Love Story* and the death camps to the same sentimental treatment.[16]

But it is not certain that a movie any less shallow, a movie any more accurate or discerning in method, would have made any difference at all in the matter. It is even quite likely that had true images been shown in place of this trashy flight of fancy, we still would not have been protected against the ravages of the Holocaust effect. For with this show and all the hype surrounding its broadcast, throughout all the countries in the West the massacre of the Jews entered into the realm of spectacle.

And what does ideology's analysis tell us when it blossoms into the critique of spectacle? That images are blinding at the very moment that they let us see—that their realism is an imposture, that they substitute the false for the true, the incidental for the important, and phony unanimities for real divisions. Since the programming of *Holocaust*, and by the very reason of its success, this particular discourse also applies to the gas chambers.[17]

Which suddenly gives an air of modernity and a formidable resonance to Faurisson's protests against "the colossal force of official means of disseminating information." Stigmatizing "Saint Television," mocking the media and its incessant lies, Faurisson was merely applying an already banal criticism to a subject that was still taboo. *Holocaust* did away with the taboo: since the spectacle is the totalitarianism characteristic of democracies, is questioning an event coddled by the media not evidence of a healthy, demystifying, antitotalitarian reaction?[18]

It is not a matter of pleading here for a return to innocence—innocence of the public invited to sacrifice all critical thinking only to founder more deeply in the contemplation of images; innocence of the spectacle, that neutral, diaphanous mediator that, without ever distorting a thing, would content itself with a scrupulous respect, a scrupulous reflection, of current events throughout the world. No one can deny the daily reality of propaganda, even and especially when it is disguised as objectivity and renounces the slogan (which is too crude, too vulgar) in favor of the more discreet but also more lasting refinements of clandestine persuasion.

The media offer possibilities of control and influence on which no power, despite even its most fundamental principles, can completely turn its back.

But of this much at least we must be conscious: the *langue de bois*—that petrification of the word, that degradation of thought into cliché—does not ensue from propaganda as such but from a perverted critique of propaganda. The most thorough brainwashing does not close the mind off as effectively as the presumptuous practice of exegesis, which, as a result of conditioning, challenges all events that fail to fit neatly into the theory, all facts that are troubling to the system.

In view of the random violence an event may perpetrate, and faced with the power to break and enter concealed within it, simple stupidity will not do: no matter how fixed or stereotyped they may be, the stock formula and the generally accepted idea can give way in the shock of a distressing experience or revelation. In short, the trite is fragile. What is indestructible, though, is war logic and its ability to convert chance into intention and to transform the disturbance caused by the unforeseen into a maneuver by the Adversary. The lesson to be learned from this is that it is easier to escape the real through interpretation than it is through endless repetition of the same old line. This explains why revolutionary self-assuredness can take on "the serenity of imbeciles" that so fascinated the author of *Bouvard and Pécuchet* and the *Dictionary of Accepted Ideas* and beat it at its own game: "Stupidity is something unshakable; nothing can attack it without being broken. It has the quality of granite, hard and resistant."[19]

It is, in fact, the comical tragedy of the twentieth century that in its effort to combat bourgeois ideology—the very same one that writers of the nineteenth century called

53

stupidity—the present era invented a more granitic language, a mode of thought even more unshakable.

Therein lies the *disturbing familiarity* of "revisionism." What is most insane about this method—the abolition of the real—is also what is most ordinary about it. Whatever criticisms are addressed to it must be generalized to any number of those who speak a *langue de bois*, because they have given the last word to the struggle and have placed history under the jurisdiction of a military model.

3

The Disillusioned Generation
A Portrait of the Duped
as Nonbelievers

I no longer entertain any illusions: that is just when they begin. Karl Kraus

A character from *The Sleepwalkers*, the great novel by Hermann Broch, was surprised to see so many men of different eras all living at the same time and even managing to be the same age as each other. To cross paths with individuals who are not one's contemporaries is to experience the bizarre phenomenon of a *time quake*: the smooth surface of time opens up to reveal several historicities where the deceptive gentleness of a unique and linear history once prevailed. Often it takes only the slightest disruption—a trip, the crossing of a bridge, or a conversation—to experience this peculiar impression of rupture and exile. And if one is so insistent on invoking the atmosphere or the spirit of the age, it is perhaps because it is so convenient to do so in order to escape the uneasiness brought about by the fragmentation of chronological unity and the studding of time with a multitude of temporal stars.

But what is even stranger, even more stunning, is to see at times so many men of different eras gathering together beneath a single banner, defending the same cause in the name of divergent if not incompatible principles. Normalization of the genocide is one of these exceptional occurrences. The mystique of the fight, and revolutionary dogma: we have seen the stiffening of these two traditions produce "revision-ism." We will now see this discourse gain followers or, at the very least, sympathizers among the very people who put down their weapons and who, in an effort to expiate their younger years, have since become obsessed with a single objective: the dissolution of all dogmas.

Actually, one word opened the hearts (and failing that, the ears) of the most reticent to the principle of negation. This magic word that need only be uttered to dispel the mistrust of skeptics, this value word that transcends the fiercest dis-putes, this program word from which no one can hide with-out risking intellectual disqualification, this manna word that changes dubious battles into philosophical epics—this word is the word *taboo*. Pronounce its two syllables, and the old communes with the new, the modern with the post-modern. Oddly reconciled, the rock-hard *langue de bois* of complete revolution and the soft language of post-Marxism fraternize in one big liberating fervor.

Faurisson's stubborn determination to deprive a commu-nity of its memory first provokes stupefaction, followed by indignation as the movement begins to spread. And by a truly infernal coincidence of fate, this wound feeds the phe-nomenon and aggravates the spread of the disease. For whether it remains purely declarative or turns to repression, the suffering is necessarily exteriorized as a *scandal*. And as day follows night, is it not true that every time someone has the misfortune (or the courage) to tackle a subject that is *taboo*, public opinion rises up and a scandal erupts? And if a taboo is weighing down upon the genocide, should we not drop everything and lift the taboo, regardless of the cost, in order to submit the event to the healthy indiscretion of scientific inquiry? In this way, "revisionism" proves to be as persuasive as its discourse is inhuman. Its victims' very suffering confers the appearance of transgression on slander and the beauty of sacrilege on injustice.

Ecrasez l'infâme, no pity for the obscurantists! The negation claims to be in keeping with the glorious tradition of the Enlightenment, Faurisson-Voltaire is fighting against dogmatism, and because he dares to violate religious prohibitions, he is braving the fearsome coalition of sanctimonious hypocrites and outmoded thinkers. And this despite the outrages of intolerance, in order to ensure the final victory of reason over the irrationality of belief or the argument of authority.

For the moment, everything is frozen on account of the efforts by those who want to embalm memories, to impose respect for an image of history that is not particularly intelligible. Certain people are not far from believing that we are witnessing the birth of a new religion, that of the Holocaust, with its dogmas and its priests.[1]

In their own view, the negators are thus martyrs of the *Aufklärung*, tortured victims of progress, modern-day Galileos. On one side, they contend, there are the votaries of Memory, rejecting as profanation any attitude other than piety and observance. On the other side, a handful of idolsmashers is proposing the substitution of a free and open investigation in place of the *commemorative* relationship with the Nazi episode. These courageous iconoclasts are braving the dominant if not crushing conformity with the sole purpose of liberating the reality of the concentration camps from clerical authority that, in the name of remembrance, is keeping watch and holding science in check. They would deprive the genocide of the sacred respect that protects it from scrutiny and would instead expose it to that objectification constituted by the work of the historian, although such an accomplishment means seeing it lose its standing as an exceptional occurrence in the process.

Hence the opposition of Memory and History, in a clearcut, archetypical duel: passionate Memory and impassive History—Memory inclined to myth and insidiously misdirected by superstition; and rational, incorruptible, inquisitive History, with no use for sentiment. This spectacular antithesis rests upon a distortion of collective memory. By speaking with a harmful vulgarity (to which we shall return) about priests of the Holocaust or dignitaries of suffering, one reduces the passion of remembrance to an idolatrous cult and a prostration of intelligence. But remaining faithful to the genocide is more complex, more demanding than this caricature. It does not consist of bowing to an event that is untouchable, absolute, forever set in its mournful eternity; it does not transform the Jews into *pleureurs*, in both the mechanical and pathetic senses of the term.[2] The impossible refusal to forget (this necessary war is lost in advance) is but another name for the will to know what happened, in all its detail and design. Learn the names of the camps, their specific characteristics, and the way they functioned internally. Gain as precise and as detailed an idea as possible of the horror in its *everyday* reality. Overcome all sense of modesty; do not give in to lyricism; and imagine how extermination was carried out, its technical problems, its constraints, and its vicissitudes. Discover the *politics* of barbarity, and learn its rules: prison hierarchy, rivalries wisely maintained by the authorities between the detainees of various nations, between the Greens (common criminals) and the Reds (political prisoners). Interrogate the survivors. Read the accounts of the ghetto to destroy once and for all the myth of the victims' passivity and to understand that desperately trying to stay alive in a place where one is supposed to die upsets the plans of absolute oppression and constitutes an act of resistance. Whether the positivists like it or not, the genocide is not the stage for a conflict between faithfulness and knowledge. Jews born after the catastrophe are not afraid of turning over this portion of history to historians but to symbols, to these few majestic words, *Auschwitz*, *Holocaust*, the *Six Million*, which, while claiming to sum it all up, lead to amnesia by way of celebration. Three or four words for a whole genocide—what economy! What one thinks is an allegiance to memory is really only laziness, a growing lapse of memory disguised as devotion. If a contradiction exists, it is not between Memory and History; it is between Memory and Metaphors that gradually replace the event of which they are the reminder.

We have to know: such is the task incumbent upon those who come *after*. We cannot settle for emphatic abstractions that designate evil without giving any real idea of it. But (and perhaps this is the true specificity of Memory), once the historian's work has released us from the traps of rhetoric and the law of least effort, we also must temper our knowledge with humbleness. "And how, in fact, can one accept not to know? We read books on Auschwitz. The wish of all, in the camps, the last wish: know what has happened, do not forget, and at the same time never will you know."[3]

Never will we know: within that catastrophic experience is something intransmissible, a murky, dark side that indefinitely feeds the will to know but that must be protected against the ever-arrogant, ever-mystified belief that everything has been brought to light and that nothing incommunicable remains. It is as if the deportees' testimony, as prolific and detailed as it may be, were enveloped in silence. It tells all, and at the same time, it warns us against the illusion that all has been said. Memory thus maligned is devoted to the assumption of silence. Is this a religion? Of course not, if by religion one means a strict piety, a blind faith, a belief independent of proof. The fact remains that Memory establishes an original sort of relationship between itself and that particular moment in history, a relationship that respects separation rather than abolishing it. Memory seeks to know about the genocide while recognizing it as unknowable, to guarantee the genocide's presence against oblivion and its distance against reductive discourses, to make the event graspable while keeping it out of our reach, to welcome it without assimilating it. In these ways, no doubt, Memory can be said to be religious, the very opposite of obscurantism.

The "revisionist" tour de force will therefore have been to push the *reductive spirit* to its ultimate consequences and, as we might have known, to call it the *spirit of Enlightenment*. Now, the world in which we live is populated to a large extent by ex-believers or, to be more precise, by people subjugated by that particular image of themselves: certain that they once believed and assured that they no longer do, shamefully or nostalgically recounting the itinerary that led them from utopia to disenchantment. Their living god was named Mao, Castro, Giap, Cleaver, Jerry Rubin, or Che Guevara. These idols were the incarnation of the true revolution, the orgasmic, idyllic, and subversive one as opposed to its degraded, repressive, authoritarian version. They procured for their followers the pleasures of heterodoxy and the delights of the schism. The crimes or failures of socialism did not shake their convictions; on the contrary, they fortified them, for was it not their job to extract the revolutionary essence from its disastrous realizations? They condemned capitalism in the name of its overthrow and Brezhnev's socialism in the name of the truth (or the surpassing) of socialism. Hence all doubt was blocked from entering their heart of hearts. One by one, however, the gods died off. Brutally snatched from their critical sleep, disappointed leftists swear that they will no longer raise temples to myths: they will wring the neck of ingenuity and cease to let an individual or a people do as it pleases, on the pretext that they command the prestige both of revolution and of heresy with respect to revolutionary order. Henceforth criticism resumes its rightful place, but despite all this, historical atheism has not freed us from magic spells. The present era proclaims that it has seen it all before: from now on, if a myth is to have any chance of *taking hold*, it is necessary (it is sufficient, almost) that it assume the appearance of demystification and denounce as fraud everything that contradicts its own lies. It is its incredulity that renders this disillusioned generation so permeable, so credulous in the face of "revisionist" inventions. The healthy disenchantment of recent years has produced its own fanatics. These fanatics look around at the world and see in it only universal trickery and empty theories to be deflated. The duped have become clever. From the follies of their youth they have learned this one valuable lesson: never let yourself be taken in again. They are told, "The period of Nazism is taboo," and like automatons of suspicion, they reply that the history of Nazism must be reexamined.

When it comes down to soul-searching and promises of lucidity, "demystification" is a magic word that lulls critical thinking to sleep insofar as it claims to be the very incarnation of critical thinking. No more dogmas, no more it-goes-without-saying. Everything is subject to methodical doubt and to disrespectful attention, from the most well-received ideas to the most exhilarating revolts: everything, except the *scenario of lost illusion*, which is an object of inattentive respect and becomes the fetish of the new infidels, the blind spot of their clairvoyance.

Periodically our moralists denounce the folly of the need to believe, and rightly so. But what threatens us now even more than the idolatrous instinct is the arrogance of the repentant children of 1968, the *soixante-huitards*, who have vowed to keep their eyes open and who regard the genocide as a contestable dogma because they succumbed to the adoration of false gods in the past. Burned before, they henceforth engage in a sort of transcendental snickering. And ironically, this a priori defiance makes them the naïve prey of imposture. Similar to ignorance, the certainty of no longer believing can cause as much spiritual damage as blind faith in a doctrine, class, or nation. So many former-this or ex-that are now yielding to seduction by analogy and settling scores with their past through a revision of the genocide!

There thus comes about the marriage of the "neo" and the "archeo," stranger still than the famous conjunction of the umbrella and the sewing machine. Certain people's hope is intact and their system unimpaired because they never have put it to the test of real life. Locked away in the abstract Marxism of the abolition of the wage-earning class, they denounce all instruments of domination and consider socialism's current form, liberal democracies, and fascist dictatorships all to be variations of a single fundamental barbarity: the barbarity of exploitation. Others detest these formulas and see them only as devitalized words or criminal dogmas, for these people have matured, and they refuse to disculpate the theory from its totalitarian shifts. What do the two groups have in common? The refusal to regard Nazism as an *absolute*—because, the "archeos" affirm, this type of regime must not be separated from the others, exempt from the general capitalist rule; because, say the "neos," religion begins when one disconnects an experience or an event and, for better or for worse, gives it special treatment. The proof: we and our totemic obsession with raising the revolutions of the last half-century above common history, of isolating them, of setting them apart so that we might project our idyllic dreams on their bloody reality. Who says that in the last thirty-five years the world has not been projecting its bloody nightmares on the ordinary if not idyllic reality of Nazi violence?

Marriage does not mean fusion. The "archeos" go along with Faurisson to the point of negating the gas chambers. The "neos" are more circumspect and know how to ferret out the dogma or the folly in integral "revisionism." With a high-mindedness for which they congratulate themselves, they dismiss those on both sides of the issue without favoring either one over the other. "There were gas chambers," they declare for the benefit of the ultraleft, "but no doubt not as many as you think," they quickly add, nodding at those who denounce revisionist discourse as an untruth hardly any more well-crafted than the *Protocols of the Elders of Zion*. The game ends in a tie, so the conclusion is: let history begin! Let the confrontation of ideologues give way to the work of historians! Let knowledge have its turn with the genocide and, steering clear of passions in the collectedness of science, finally tell us what happened. Did we not have to wait until the early 1970s to unlock the doors to the Occupation period and learn, in *The Sorrow and the Pity*, that France had not really resisted in the war? Yet another myth was debunked. Still reeling from the noise surrounding this most recent downfall and from the collapse of all their beliefs, those who have given up on utopia are atoning for the error of their ways by turning their doubt into a reflex that is just as conditioned as struggle was during their militant period. All acknowledged reality seems dubious to them so long as one is skillful enough to disguise it as an idol in their eyes.

It is not difficult to imagine how initiating proceedings against Faurisson affected this mode of thinking that cultivates impiety and seeks to use an irreproachable liberalism to expiate its delirium of intolerance still fresh in people's minds. Legal proceedings and condemnations moved

The Disillusioned Generation

Faurisson out of the category of maniac and into the Christ-like category of victim: his situation was validated by its judicial repercussions; his argumentation suddenly seemed interesting not for any intrinsic qualities but because it had stirred public opinion and provoked a general outcry. The newspaper *Libération* (which, in many respects, is the daily manifesto of the disillusioned generation) could therefore say: "At the time of all the debates, it was actually possible to verify the extent to which the Nazi period was still *taboo*, with every challenge of such and such point from that period looking like a veritable *sacrilege*."[4]

Automatic demystification culminated here in pure mythology or, to borrow from Roland Barthes's classic analysis, in the "loss of history." Once it went to court, the Faurisson affair lost all proper reality: its difference was eliminated; its originality disappeared in that unchanging archetype, the witch hunt, of which it is now just the docile illustration. The trial conformed to the Trial in its inquisitorial truth, and the tribune was merely the accidental site where the drama of eternal Censorship and Repression in oneself was played out. The result: suspicion about orthodoxy henceforth weighs heavily on our present-day knowledge of Nazism. Thanks to the Faurisson trial, the disillusioned generation has constituted as *dogma* certain essential works—books by Dawidowicz, Hilberg, Langbein—whose titles and existence are no doubt unknown to the very people now contesting them.[5]

THE NEW LAISSEZ-FAIRE

Ahead of these obligations or these acknowledgments of interest, I place a perpetual, rightful obligation that is subject to no exceptions, that can neither expand nor diminish because it is always total, that is imperative for small reviews and large newspapers alike, that cannot vary according to circulation or competition or purposes: the obligation to tell the truth.

To tell the truth, the whole truth, and nothing but the truth; to tell the stupid truth in a stupid way, the boring truth in a boring way, the sad truth in a sad way: that is what we proposed to do more than twenty months ago, and not only for questions of doctrine and method, but also, and especially, for action. We have almost succeeded at it. Must we give up on it now? Péguy, *Lettre du provincial,* 5 January 1900

It is a strange thing, this Faurisson affair. Certain intransigent Marxists offer him the support of dogma; others offer him their complacency out of hatred for dogmatism. The first group, under the name of historical materialism, subordinates reality to a transcendental reasoning: knowing or believing that they know the true moving forces of the evolving course of events, they see within facts the continuously reiterated confirmation of that fundamental truth. Taking the point of view of the totality of things, they uncover the meaning of events by incorporating them into the social process, by resituating them in the global logic of which they partake: the antagonism between the bourgeoisie and the working class. With the Final Solution, a contradiction brutally erupts between the law of history and history itself. Unruffled, our dogmatic contingent chooses revolutionary truth over perceptible reality and assures domination of the whole over its parts by chastising that demoniac, the genocide.

Conversely the disillusioned generation is experiencing the erosion of doctrines, the twilight of the idols, the breakdown of all beliefs. Having ended up distrustful and unbelieving, this generation identifies thinking with exercising suspicion. Now modest, it is loath to categorize peoples, nations, or individuals as either obstacles to or instruments of the movement of history. It is a healthy resolution that leads to the wrack and ruin of the totality and to the rehabilitation of the learned or the experts. Penitent praxis restores to the University what it stole from it in the name of revolutionary science. The militants have played with the truth for long enough, and it now falls within the exclusive purview of the scholars, which is to say those who exhibit the *exterior signs of scientific inquiry*: a punctilious mind, an imposing bibliography, an impressive assemblage of references. Hatred of the University is thus changed into a *cult of scholarly appearance*: revision *looks serious*, and a few derisory symbols of austerity are all it takes to gain the confidence of the converted, who only a short while ago classified all works devoid of the spirit of the Revolution under the convenient heading of dominant ideology.

And skepticism extends even beyond this transfer of competence. It opens up a whole new area in which to exercise one's right to a free opinion: the past. Indeed, the rediscovered democratic ideal requires that wherever possible, pluralism be substituted for the reign of a single truth. In keeping with this notion, putting the gas chambers into doubt is hailed as a giant step forward—and for reasons that are strictly quantitative. Where there once was only one truth, two options are now available. Two instead of one: that is what matters and not the content or the validity of opposing arguments. The individual used to be subject to evidence. With controversy he is in a position to choose. Freed from the actual event and from the passive obedience it requires, he accedes to adulthood, and exercising his supreme authority, he can mark his preference for one of two conflicting versions of history. It is a victory of the multiple over the one, of democracy over constraint, of individualism over the gregarious instinct. I am in charge of *my* truth instead of being the inert receptacle of an objective, single universal truth. Thus the traditional order of priorities is reversed: the debate is no longer a means but an end; the truth is no longer an end but a prejudice, an abuse, or an obstacle. Whatever the object might be, each point put forth in the debate rescues a bit of information from the clutches of the tyrant. Is it not the objective of power to regulate, control, and rarefy the profusion of discourses in order to reduce them in the end to one lone Word? If so, the more versions of history that circulate, the more murmurings of untruths and the more divergent opinions there are, the weaker the risks of totalitarianism become. To sustain the enterprise of negation, one alternately invokes the *academic* argument (there are credible revisionists: researchers loaded with quotations and footnotes on every page) and the *liberal* argument (the will for truth masks a will for control, which only an assiduous defense of liberty can thwart).[6]

"The only countries I know where it is said that a historical truth is eternal are totalitarian countries," one of the witnesses in Faurisson's second trial was able to say. In other words, contesting the reality of the gas chambers and substituting discussion for certainty in this domain is an act of resistance to power. The whole misunderstanding of this democratic revindication can therefore be summed up as follows: *historical truth* is confused with *metaphysical truth*; in the same angry suspension of belief, one deduces the absence of truth *in* history from the acknowledgment that there is no truth *of* history; and fact is broken down into a multitude of lies so as to put a more decisive end to unitary theories. The meaning of history (along with its murderous consequences) is countered with a mass of accounts, a chaos of opinions and interpretations whose numbers one seeks to increase despite restrictive constraints. In short, transcendence is answered with a "no holds barred"—hence the formidable blindness, the paroxysm of confusion that faults the single party for committing the sin that is the opposite of the one it commits every day. Where, if not in totalitarian countries subjugated to the reign of a single idea, is historical truth perishable and *subject to forced labor exacted by the government*? Margarete Buber-Neumann reports one of the hundreds of thousands of examples of this subjection: "A novel that the State publishing house had at first accepted, and in which H. J. described the life of a foreigner in the Soviet Union by mentioning the 1930–31 famine years, was rejected for publication with the following observation: 'There was never any famine in the Soviet Union.'"[7]

In trying thus to dismiss both the truth of fact and the truth of dogma in one fell swoop, one does not abolish this retrospective despotism; one popularizes it. The principle of "to each his own truth" transfers to individuals the privilege that totalitarian societies reserve for the State: a discretionary power over history.

It is forbidden to forbid. In its terse beauty this sentence sums up well the naïveté of a contestation that, at the very moment it believes itself to be delivering a blow to the heart of power, is merely limiting it to putting its most anodyne properties into play. Challenged as censorship and purely negative violence, the Party-State is at the same time exculpated of its worst invention: the falsification of the past. And instead of being treated as zealots, those who transcribe Big Brother and recreate his practices appear as victims of totalitarian domination.

What the Faurisson affair shows is that terror and laissez-faire are the two avatars of the same liquidation. The remedy is a variant of the evil it is supposed to cure. In the hell that is steeped in a single idea, facts are tamed and then made responsible for ratifying what is known; in the Eden spared from the archaism of historical truth, the multiplicity of opinions keeps the upper hand over facts.

The Disillusioned Generation

ADOLF STALIN?

For the Jews of Sighet, a small city in Transylvania, the spring of 1944 marked the beginning of horror—the arrival of the Nazis, the ghetto, and the departure to the camps. That night came crashing down on the town by surprise, despite the information that had made its way there two years before.

The train full of deportees had crossed the Hungarian frontier and on Polish territory had been taken in charge by the Gestapo. There it had stopped. The Jews had to get out and climb into lorries. The lorries drove toward a forest. The Jews were made to get out. They were made to dig huge graves. And when they had finished their work, the Gestapo began theirs. Without passion, without haste, they slaughtered their prisoners. Each one had to go up to the hole and present his neck. Babies were thrown up into the air and machine gunners used them as targets. This was in the forest of Galicia, near Kolomay. How had Moshe the Beadle escaped? Miraculously. He was wounded in the leg and taken for dead.[8]

Having been deported with all the foreign Jews, Moshe the Beadle had come back alone to Sighet to tell his story and the story of his companions: "I don't want money or pity. Only listen to me," but the Jews of Sighet preferred to think that he was trying to make them feel sorry for him or that he had gone crazy.

When the Jews of Vilno were informed by survivors about the massacres that the Einsatzgruppen (the special units) of the German army were perpetrating at Ponary, the area immediately surrounding their own town, they did not want to believe them: "After all, this is Europe, not the Jungle."[9]

When the Jews of Warsaw learned from emissaries from Vilno of the atrocities staged in Lithuania, they could not doubt the truth of the information. But they sought reassurance in telling themselves that they were living in the middle of Europe and that this centrality protected them from the barbarity being unleashed farther away, on the fringes, in the margins. The Jews of Holland and Denmark resorted to the same technique of denial, except that they were the ones occupying the center while Poland, the site of the genocide, represented the periphery. Supporting themselves with the illusion of this cultural geography (Europe is civilization, and we live in the heart of it) and the *pessimism* of common sense (self-interest, the supreme passion, determines all behaviors, the most virtuous and the most criminal alike, and a Germany at war is in need of slaves), the designated victims put up a fierce resistance against the news of what was going to be their fate.

As of 1942, throughout the whole of Europe, rumors had broken the wall of silence, fragmentary but numerous and detailed accounts had disclosed the "terrifying secret" of the Final Solution. People's consciousness nevertheless did all it could to hide from this revelation; the truth floated back and forth between ignorance and knowledge. This refusal to believe, which some misleadingly call passivity, undoubtedly made the Nazis' task easier. But it must be said that this project of total, expeditious annihilation of a dispersed population required a strictly unimaginable technology and had no precedent in either the anti-Semitism of the pogroms or the modern development of forced work camps.

Consciousness was stupid, in the strict sense of the term. There was no place within it for entertaining the idea of a process of extermination that exceeded the bounds of all categories of common immorality, the workings of self-interest and perversion alike. The professionalization of the massacre, that strange intersection of absolute barbarity and extreme civilization, constituted a crime unheard of ever before. The reasoning characteristic of utilitarian thought was foreign to it; and as for sadism, it suddenly seemed to have no pertinence whatsoever. The Final Solution defied explanation in terms of instinct and psychological release since it was not *bestiality* that it was applying to murder but *efficiency*, the behavior principle of all normal human beings, that "logical frame of mind directed toward its object, and only toward its object, looking neither to the right nor the left," in which as early as 1930 Hermann Broch recognized the style of the modern era.[10]

It would be tempting to think that forty years later we are witnessing an analogous phenomenon of repudiation. An innocent generation, wrapped in a cocoon of oblivion, reads books and discovers the factories of death and the invention of chambers of asphyxiation. Is their surprise really all that surprising? And when a scandal turns their surprise into incredulity, is it not a sign of a resurgence? Is it not the stupor of the genocide's contemporaries repeating itself in their descendants? With the passage of time, do the gas chambers not return to the realm of the unreal because they are not the least bit plausible, because even the darkest, most cynical vision of humanity is powerless to explain that process by which the useless becomes a viable commodity—that unleashing of irrationality within an ultrarational framework, that enterprise of annihilation raised to an absolute level and focused, to the exclusion of all other considerations, on beating its own records in the radical spirit of its own particular logic?

Part of the new generation would thus be bolstering "revisionism" with *common sense*. The thesis is an appealing one, and a reassuring one as well, for it establishes the filiation of those coming after the war to those who witnessed the event. The link is the very humanity of man in confrontation with a reality that shatters its notion of the impossible. For the love of humanity, if only the negation of the gas chambers were a matter of probability taking revenge against the truth, of conscience revolting against its own disappearance! Unfortunately, it is nothing of the sort. And the pessimism of Georges Wellers remains distorted by indulgence:[11] "The more time that passes, the greater the risk that the gas chambers will seem unreal and 'impossible' to the generations unfamiliar with the Nazi period."[12]

This picture of gloom is still much too rosy. Negation has the future on its side, but such fragility of history is not a result of the excessiveness or the monstrousness of Nazism; it stems from *its difference*. We spoke earlier about the members of what we called the disillusioned generation. Two axioms have dissipated their revolutionary ardor: Stalin is no better than Hitler, and Marxist ideology cannot be fully exonerated for the errors of Stalin's ways. In some people, as we have seen, this disabused acknowledgment leads to an attitude of laissez-faire: since Marxism is false, nothing is true. What one personally used to adore is thrown into the fire along with the god that is currently burning, namely the objectivity of the real. Others, perhaps in greater numbers, merely change their a priori by switching allegiance to another banner.

In the days when the hopes and torments of progressivism dominated the intellectual left, only the right talked about *totalitarian* society. It was a convenient way of looking only at fortuitous similarities and grouping fascism and communism together under a single concept—namely the dissolution of all moral heritage and the very fulfillment of morality. Denying man and developing man: the two undertakings could not be confused, except to deprive the left of all standards and all justification for existence. It became evident—and such is disillusionment, such is the lesson of the waning twentieth century—that the two opposite paths led to the same unique form of oppression and annihilation. With Solzhenitsyn it certainly seems to be the case that the idea of totalitarianism has defeated or marginalized the final acts of resistance to it. An antiauthoritarian left is now trying to come into being on the rubble of progressivism. But disillusionment has its neophytes, the temple is still under construction, and already guards are posted. For the supercilious trustees of this new truth, it is a sacrilege not to compare but to distinguish Hitler's side from Stalin's. The gas chambers are therefore *suspect* because they are *specific*.[13] And these logical antitotalitarians will accept the reality of the Nazi gassings when it is proven to them that the same thing happened in the Gulag. Until then, like Jean-Gabriel Cohn-Bendit,[14] they have their doubts, and this incredulity is not a product of stupor but of resentment. What was so kindly regarded as a revolt of common conscience is in fact an ideologue's bitterness toward an unclassifiable, anarchical, insolent fact that seems to fly in the face of knowledge that is all the more incontestable for its being marked with the seal of disillusionment.

With the Soviet Union's return to the great democratic fold, it was necessary that there be some absolute difference between Stalinist and Nazi totalitarianism. A Stalinist camp had nothing to do with a Nazi extermination camp, even if people died there too.

The Nazi regime, whose symbol is the gas chambers, is perceived as absolute evil, it goes beyond the bounds of history.[15]

Stalinized Marxism established a priori what was real, and instead of decoding experience, it "fit events, persons or actions under consideration into prefabricated molds."[16] But the method stays the same if all you do is choose a different mold. The negation of the gas chambers is the moment in which petrified, mineralized antitotalitarian discourse terrorizes and disposes of the particularities or excesses of the real. Cohn-Bendit sees totalitarianism as constituting an underlying design, and on this basis he engages in an inflexible initiative of elimination. The gas chambers are sacrificed to its unifying fury and are omitted from the Nazi genocide because they hinder the identification between Auschwitz and the Gulag.

On the subject of official Marxism, Jean-Paul Sartre wrote, "Specific determinations awaken the same suspicions regarding the theory that individual persons do regarding reality." Raised to the status of absolute knowledge, permanently set in a *langue de bois*, the critique of Stalinism mimics its object and reacts to all the licentiousness of history like a bureaucrat exasperated by an infraction of the rules or a slip in behavior.

We are beginning to catch on to this tune of equivalence. In the negation of the gas chambers, the same hatred of the event is always at work, as is the same refusal to differentiate fascism and democracy in the one case and Stalin and Hitler in the other. David Rousset wrote, "Normal men do not know that everything is possible." One will therefore conclude that contemporary men are not normal men, for they are bombarded with enough information to know that anything is possible. Yet they fail to resist the temptation to classify all the different manifestations of barbarity under a single heading.

Complete assimilation of the two concentration camp systems can be maintained only with the heavy cost of tremendous historical deafness. What it implies is that the Soviets made up and propagated the myth of the gassing of the Jews to make their own repression of the Jews look inoffensive in comparison and to make the Gulag seem like a picnic, like a boy scout camp in Siberia—like a somewhat strict summer camp and nothing more. But such Machiavellianism is contradictory to Stalinist propaganda that minimized the Final Solution from the beginning on. Stalin, the first "revisionist." It was in Russia that the systematic massacre of the Jews began. To the obvious surprise of the Einsatzgruppen, the victims had no idea of the fate awaiting them. They did not have to do as their fellow Jews in Poland did and resort to incredulity to defend themselves against what they knew. They were unaware of even the first thing, for the Russian press had kept them ignorant, being careful to maintain silence concerning the measures that Hitler had already taken against the "germ-race" (*peuple-microbe*) in his own country. The German-Russian nonaggression pact demanded it! And when on 6 January 1942 a note signed by Molotov and addressed to the allied governments denounced the monstrous acts committed by the German authorities, no mention was made of the particular destiny reserved for the Jews, that is, the desire for total extermination that was already operating against them. Why? Because it was a matter of building up hatred and mobilizing energy against the invader. And murdering the Jews would most likely sit quite well with nations such as the Ukraine, Lithuania, and Latvia, which were already susceptible to guarantees of independence promised by the Nazi occupier. Pro-Hitler, then anti-Hitler, Stalinist politics stayed the same: the special treatment inflicted upon those whom Hitler called the "parasites living on the bodies of other peoples" was not taken into account. And de-Stalinization never affected this legendary moment of Soviet history. As concerns the war, invariance of the Party line, not its relaxation, prevailed as it continued in its refusal to isolate the damage done to Soviet citizens of Jewish origin from that done to the rest.

It is true that in his antitotalitarian zeal, Jean-Gabriel Cohn-Bendit pushes terrorism to the point of the pure and simple abolition of facts that dare to challenge his a priori principles governing history. The most widespread negation relinquishes this position. Nuanced, measured, and impartial, it does not contest the *existence* but the *importance* of the gas chambers. "Yes," say these new wise men, "the Nazis used Zyklon B to annihilate those who they had decided were subhuman. Yes, perhaps. Yes, certainly. But what do these lugubrious, chemical details matter? Millions of people died in Hitler's occupied Europe. They were exterminated or subjected to neglect. They died, slowly, of hunger or fatigue; or they died, methodically, from being gassed. It was the same crime. All the fine distinctions serve only to distract us from that horrible truth or to seek extenuating circumstances for the supreme Leader of the revolution."

For this version of antitotalitarian thought, the materiality of fact does not count. Even worse, it blurs the principal information; it torpedoes the symbolic truth that emerges from the charnel houses, namely the relatedness (or perhaps we should go so far as to say the twinship) of the two great monsters born of this century. The gas chambers are thus not declared void but are reduced to an incidental technology (used only on a certain occasion). They fall into the category of the unusable, the secondary, and the *nonsignifying*.

And through a turnaround that in and of itself justifies the writing of this book, the same people who rebel against the arbitrariness or the arrogance of separating the contingent (the means employed) from the essential (the genocide) are called upon to justify their opinion. Are they not, in their morbid fetishism, seeking to postpone or compromise the effort to expose the totalitarian imposture? Or are Jews absorbed in malediction and solitude trying to shelter their heartbreak from our common history and to fashion for themselves a massacre unlike all others in modern times? What an admirable paradox: to put stock in fact is to scorn history, while to scorn fact or proclaim its insignificance is to accede to consciousness of the workings of history. Marxist culture and the type of thinking that deposes it have something in common: they both give the same bureaucratic or regulatory meaning to the word "history."

It is now easier to see the discrepancy or the misunderstanding that exists between Faurisson and the affair that bears his name. As he himself put it, Faurisson wants to deliver some "good news" to humanity. To free it from remorse. To acquit it of the inexplicable murder of which it has been accusing itself for the last forty years. To let it sleep easy again and to give it back that good conscience of which the human slaughterhouses of Chelmno, Sobibor, Auschwitz, and Treblinka seemed to deprive it forevermore. Faurisson is speaking to people in the gentle language of innocence. And no one is ready to listen to it, except perhaps a marginal, discredited France that still entertains the Vichy ideal. There is, however, an audience for the harsh discourse that rejects attempts at absolution and is used not to erase the Blame but to see that it is shared equally. Irked by the Pétainism in the notion that "tout le monde il est beau, tout le monde il est gentil,"[17] proponents of the negation are calling for a *better distribution of the bad news*. It is not so that they can exonerate men that these prosecutors deny the gas chambers or consider them to be a residual phenomenon, a minor event, a totally useless by-product of thought; their purpose is a better distribution of guilt. There is plenty of Blame to go around everywhere; the trick is knowing how to expose the true instigators of crime. For antitotalitarians, it is essential that Russia be held culpable of crimes attributed to Nazi Germany; for supporters of the Third World, American imperialism must be; and for extreme leftists, capital must be. Everything that stands in the way of this condemnation is excluded from the real or banished from what is known.

The Faurisson affair is therefore situated at the core of our intellectual lives. It is a crossroads where all modern forms of contempt for the facts meet and coalesce: Marxist dogmatism, antitotalitarian dogmatism, and finally nihilism and its jolly principle that the world has become a sham. But the hero of the affair does not put stock in any one of these philosophies. We should therefore forget about Faurisson if we are to recognize the true extent of the phenomenon and uncover the *crises of understanding* that underlie the inanity of the anecdote.

Forget about Faurisson and examine instead the person of whom he is but a pale imitation, the mere transcriber. The true central figure in the affair is a man named Paul Rassinier. A survivor of Buchenwald and Dora, he was, as Vidal-Naquet notes, the first one to have "shown in systematic fashion that no genocide occurred."[18] As a result of his provocations and his doctoring of the facts, Faurisson is hardly even presentable anymore. For Rassinier, however, it is just the opposite. As a former resister, deportee, and revolutionary, he has what it takes to impress people. Who could imagine a more irreproachable record for the inspirer of the negation? Rassinier will continue to stimulate reductive discourses long after Faurisson has faded into oblivion.

RASSINIER, THE GOODTHINKER OF BUCHENWALD

It is in homage to George Orwell that Solzhenitsyn calls them "goodthinkers." They make up that category of zeks (detainees of the Gulag) who, though surprised at their own deportation, nevertheless applauded the system that made it possible and defended the Soviet regime with the same exaltation they had when they were free. "It is impossible to imagine to oneself a goodthinker who for one moment in a daydream would let out a peep about the death of Stalin."[19] These management-level Communists knew how to keep their convictions out of the reach of their experience, even when that experience was as sad and unpredictable as their arrest. They continued to commune with power even when power rode roughshod over them. How did they do it? They blamed their imprisonment on the schemes of the German secret service or on "historical necessity." These explanations exonerated the revolution; and inasmuch as they declared Stalin not guilty of arbitrary repression, they also white-washed him, that shining sun that nothing must eclipse. "Loyalty?" asks Solzhenitsyn; "in our view it is just plain pigheadedness." And he adds:

Let life gush over them, surge over them, or even roll over them with wheels—still they won't let it into their heads! They won't accept it, as though it weren't happening at all! This reluctance to change anything inside their own brains, this simple inability to make a critical assessment of their life's experience, is what they pride themselves on! Prison must not influence their world out-look! Camp must not influence it! What they stood upon before, they will continue to stand by now! We . . . are Marxists! We . . . are materialists! How can we possibly change because we landed in prison by sheer chance?[20]

The world has come to know this stubbornness through recent history. With so many victims of Stalinism having cried out "Long live the Party!" from the gallows, we have become accustomed to that strange ideological promiscuity between the tortured and his executioner. What is unusual, though, is to see a survivor of the Nazi camps devoting the rest of his life to rehabilitating Hitler's Germany. Paul Rassinier is this exception: a goodthinker from Buchenwald.

It is true that even before it liquidated human beings, Hitlerism liquidated the very concept of humanity. Which prohibited the detainee and his guard, the representatives of two different species, from fraternizing in a single ideal. Nazism annihilated its victim in the name of values that these victims could not, under any circumstances, internalize. A metaphysical gap separated the oppressor from the oppressed. And Rassinier is not seeking to fill in the gap. It is not the unrecognized Aryan within him that protests against his own fate while otherwise glorifying the racial politics of the Reich. Unlike orthodox thinkers on the Soviet side, he is not an adherent of the philosophy of his masters. What he does have in common with the hardheads described by Solzhenitsyn is the *arrogance of ideology*. Rassinier is the "imperforable" man. Sealed off completely from all outside threats, his autarchic vision of the world holds up despite his real-life experience and the contradictions and refutations it presents. Rassinier returned to France physically destroyed and mentally unchanged. The violence that had been unleashed on his body had failed to gain access to his mind. The atrocities skirted and endured each day did not get the better of his pacifism. This broken man, a miracle both pitiful and comical, had not understood the first thing: as ardent a supporter of Munich afterwards as before, the author of *The Lie of Ulysses* refused to see any sort of originality within Nazism and thereby became the apologist for a system that had subjected him to torture. There is in Rassinier a certain fanaticism of thought, and regardless of even the most terrible obstacles, it manages to eliminate all difference between the Allies and the Nazis, between World War I and World War II, between the camps of the twentieth century and other forms of coercion or enslavement developed over the ages.

Le casse-pipe:[21] the Celinian title evoking the battlefront says it all and says above all that after 1914, war is a black hole into which everything meaningful is swallowed up and disappears, an abominable mystery that has nothing more to show us than the absurdity of the world. The First World War was the insane carnage that put an end to the values of war, whether they were national, ethical, or just adventurous. Henceforth nothing excused such violence—not the esthetics of challenge, not the cause being defended. It was not a question of risking one's life for the beauty of the gesture or the grandeur of an idea, "it was a question of wading through the shit with the rats" (Emmanuel Berl).[22]

In a fit of obstinacy that cannot be fully explained, Rassinier remained true to the lesson of World War I even at the heart of that new absolute phenomenon, the concentration camp world. If he describes his experience in all its detail, if he works to conceptualize it and thematize it, it is not for the purpose of communicating it; it is so he can eliminate it as experience and rid it of everything about it that falls outside the category of the same and defies the nature of repetition. He does not glorify the ss out of fascination or any sort of masochism; he trivializes them with the sole intent of inscribing one war within another and of attributing all behaviors—those of the victim and those of the executioner, those of the German soldiers and those of their adversaries—to the same unreasonable abjectness: "There can be no war without concentration camps, without Oradours on both sides, and without lieutenant colonels of the Eichmann type who are equally obedient and zealous on both sides."[23]

The novelty of the event is absorbed in the perfection of the type. There is nothing to note, nothing special in any case, nothing worse than the bellicose cruelty practiced throughout the ages, throughout the world: such is the conclusion to which Rassinier would lead the reader by writing down the tale of his personal suffering. Adopting a faulty piecemeal logic, he supports his thesis with two series of contradictory arguments:

(1) The Nazi camps are like the others. "There were camps in ancient times, in the Middle Ages, and in modern times.

Why would you expect the contemporary era to be an exception?" True, other witnesses affirm being separated from other men by an experience that is impossible to communicate. They say they "plodded along for years in the uncanny realm of bankrupt dignities."[24] They say too that in this annihilation everything foundered, and they experienced the interruption of history. Finally, they say that what is new and as yet still mysterious about the Nazi machine is that it turned atrocity into the norm. Those witnesses, warns Rassinier, are liars, windbags, pretentious frauds. And now suddenly he is a psychologist and gives a quasi-Freudian name to this tendency of theirs. These surviving braggarts are suffering "from a complex that might be labeled the lie of Ulysses, from which all men, and consequently all inmates, suffer. Humanity needs an element of the fantastic in the bad as well as in the good, in the ugly as well as in the beautiful."[25]

(2) The Nazi camps are nothing like the other camps. Terrible things happened. Who is to blame? The *Häftlingsführung*, the detainees' autonomous administration. By dividing in order to conquer, by introducing the command/obedience system into the relationships between detainees themselves, the ss delegated a portion of their powers to certain inmates. According to Rassinier, these cruel, ill-intentioned executants are responsible for the chaos, the noise, and the furor that reigned in the camp. The regulations were strict but just. Unfortunately the stewardship failed to follow them: orders were altered; various sorts of trafficking aggravated the disparity between the camp's rank and file and its aristocracy; the kapos abused their power; and the ss were betrayed. That explains why Sparta became a hell. "As for myself," says Rassinier, "I am convinced that within the limits resulting from the fact of war, nothing prevented the detainees who directed us, commanded us, kept watch over us, and supervised us from making life in the camp something

that would have closely resembled the picture of it the Germans presented through intermediaries to people seeking information."[26]

But the gas chambers? It seems difficult to attribute their invention to the detainees' sadism or to find an equivalent to them in the concentration camps that, to hear Rassinier tell it, flourish under all the governments around the world. There were no gas chambers at Buchenwald, but their existence at Auschwitz is enough to undermine all undertakings to normalize the Nazi regime. These human slaughterhouses are a stain on the monochromatic landscape of universal oppression. They resist all leveling, and they are an insult to the principle of similarity. Sensing the threat, Rassinier goes on to speak of the "irritating" question of the gas chambers. This extraordinary qualifier is a tacit admission. Rassinier is nervous, aggravated. He feels attacked in his system, wounded in his *Weltanschauung* by an unforeseen problem. Rassinier's anger is the rage inherent in ideology when history suddenly throws it off balance. But the deportee who learned to tame his own experience is not a man to admit defeat. All the books he wrote after *The Lie of Ulysses* are devoted to putting the extermination into doubt.

At first Rassinier would say, "My opinion on the gas chambers? There were some, not as many as you think. There were also exterminations by this means, not as many as has been said."[27] At a later stage Rassinier is more self-assured. He no longer quibbles over the number and refuses to concede anything: these murders simply did not take place. The irreducible is reduced; the difference evaporates into myth or rumor. All that is left is the war, its eternal ferocity and its innumerable victims. There is nothing new under the sun. The ideologist simultaneously regains his calm and his convictions.[28]

The Disillusioned Generation

Thus all roads to the negation lead back to Rassinier. He is the point of convergence for the most foreign ideologies and the most incompatible systems of thought. Everyone who is irritated by the *Nazi difference* owes a debt of gratitude to this grand precursor. With filial piety, the far left is retracing the trajectory of the revolutionary militant. After ten years in the Communist Party, Rassinier was expelled in 1932. Like Monatte, like Souvarine, he wanted to defend the principle of internationalism against an organization that had betrayed it in order to put itself in the service of the new czars. His natural family was therefore the leftist opposition that abounded outside the Party in the 1930s. In 1934, after the February riots, Rassinier joined the sfio, sided first with the revolutionary left of Marcel Pivert, then adopted the pacifist tendency of Paul Faure.[29] An ardent supporter of Munich, Rassinier denounced the Sacred Union and the imperialist war up to the end. But unlike many others, he did not go from supporting Munich to participating in the Collaboration. After lengthy deliberation Rassinier chose the Resistance. It was a choice without any illusions since in his eyes few things distinguished the opposing camps: the Russians and the Germans had raised slavery to the level of a system of government, while the Anglo-Americans (allied with the Russians) symbolized the regime of attenuated slavery. What could be expected from an Allied victory? Nothing, if not that, weakened and exhausted by war, the two sides would need to catch their breath before throwing themselves on one another.

Only while they were catching their breath did Candasse glimpse the possibility of a positive outcome to man's destiny, provided man knew how to turn the possibility to good use. And it was with these thoughts in mind that he accorded favorable consideration to the Land of the Angles and to the People of the Far Side.

But with a victory of the Führer being conceivable only under the same conditions, it was scarcely any more frightening to him.[30]

Upon his arrest Rassinier was tortured by the Gestapo and then spent two years at Buchenwald. This "goodthinker" speaks a less orthodox language than the disciples of La Vieille Taupe who feverishly republish him. In his treatment of *le "diamat"* [dialectical materialism], he takes liberties that border on sacrilege. His brand of Marxism does not scorn sweeping syntheses and seems even to take delight in the idea of an eternal socialism beginning with the Essenes and continuing through the present day. But who will dare to show the slightest disdain for him? A victim of fascist violence is denouncing antifascism. This unhoped-for survivor brings the "logico-Communists" a countertestimony that allows them to turn a deaf ear to all other accounts.

As for those who long for a return of the Reich, they cannot believe their eyes. This man in striped pajamas, this decorated Resistance member actually goes so far as to hold the Jews responsible for the war! In 1914 there was the assassination in Sarajevo; in 1938 the "Jew" Grynzpan assassinated Ernst Von Rath, third secretary of the German embassy in Paris. Each war, Rassinier explains, had its inaugural murder.

And in this way he recalls the cliché so popular in Paris in the late thirties: the image of the warlike Jew. A headline from *L'Action française* of the period reads "No War for the Jews." This was also the view held by the pacifist left disgusted with Léon Blum and his warmongering, although it was based on different arguments and more cautious consideration.

In the Socialist Party, the following story circulated by word of mouth. One day, Paul Faure, who was secretary-general, who had left the direction of his newspaper to Léon Blum, and who had not set foot there in quite a while, reappeared at the paper because he needed certain information for a report he was to submit at a con-vention. The editorial staff introduced themselves: Lévy, Meyer, Bloch, and so on. Suddenly he hears the name Dupont. A deadpan Paul Faure then exclaims, "It's terrible! Those Christians always manage to weasel their way in everywhere."[31]

Since the war, only the extreme right continues to assign blame to the Jews (and in whispered tones) by reproaching them for having ruined the chances for peace and having dragged the world into the greatest massacre in history for no better reasons than national pride and class interest. In the 1930s the cleavage between right and left was not nearly so clear, as the "joke" attributed to Paul Faure attests. And Rassinier has never wavered. Indeed it is his steadfastness and his unshakable loyalty to the convictions of his youth that have earned him his status as the hero of neofascism.

So it is that the fanatics of the disillusioned generation bow to the clear-sightedness of a survivor who, far from harboring any anti-German fixation, denounces the behavior of the Reds in the camps and that of the Soviets in the postwar world.

In my view, the Communists' maneuver was clear: by focusing on the German camps, they thought they were creating a diversion and turning the world's attention away from the twenty million people whom they were guarding in their own camps and upon whom they were imposing living conditions that eyewitness accounts by several survivors (particularly Margarete Buber-Neumann) easily proved were even worse than those experienced in the German camps.[32]

In his prophetic way Rassinier announced nearly twenty years before the fact that the antifascist left would be converted into the antitotalitarian left. In his zealous way he eliminated the only obstacle that could hinder this conversion: the gas chambers of the Nazi extermination camps.

The Disillusioned Generation

As Hannah Arendt reminds us, a purely recent phenomenon of our culture is a certain pretentiousness of thought by which we subject history to the logic of a single idea and explain the movement of the natural course of things as a unique, coherent process. This may in fact be the twentieth century's own contribution to the history of reason. And from this point of view, Rassinier is a product of the century, a true hero of our time. If in fact he is delirious, it is due to an excess of modernity; if he is mad, it is due to the total victory of ideology over common sense within him. Like Solzhenitsyn's goodthinkers, he thinks what he lives in terms of an absolute knowledge that connects each event with an eternal essence. His own life experience is no longer a test; it is a verification. Properly speaking, Rassinier has not had any experience. The worst can happen to him, and nothing happens to him. Ideology, that imperious landlord, that omnipotent host, eliminates all other forms of apprehending the real and does not allow experience to shed its own light. Is Rassinier possessed? Yes, but by that most ordinary and most contemporary demon who harnesses an event until it is tamed and politely rejects its a priori meaning.

This is obviously a far cry from the all too familiar *masochism* to which prejudice inevitably reduces relationships between master and slave. The camps are often imagined as sites of sexual activity, no doubt because they are enclosed spaces sheltered from the outside world's indiscretions. The enclosure prompts the fantasy: what is hidden from view is secret, and secrecy irresistibly conjures up lust. The "anything is possible" referred to by the deportees is translated as "everything is permitted," and an inexhaustible literature thus uncovers an erotic promiscuity between the torturer and his victim. In its vulgar form this fantasy transforms the camps into temples of pornography, into societies of debauchery where desire acts out its most extreme possibilities.

In its refined form, this fantasy defines itself as a will to know, for is it not true that the truth of the individual and the hidden meaning of history are to be found in the shadowy realm of sex? Then sexualizing the deportees' suffering in terms of masochism would further our understanding of the concentration camp universe.

One need only listen to camp witnesses instead of one's own projections in order to realize that terror, famine, and work extinguished all eroticism and desexualized the camps, and that no masochism of any kind connected the subhumans to the master race. However far-reaching its definition may be, sexual desire is not an optic that sheds any light on the workings of the ss State. The logic of concupiscence simply cannot account for what happened. Even aberrant cases such as Rassinier's fall under the heading of a different mechanism. This man so taken with (and taken over by) ideology did not like its executioners, but he liked its vision of the world. Specifically, he went as far as his ideas would take him, to the point of sacrificing his own life experience when it did not fit with the vision. He simply closed his mind and protected it from history's threat to undermine his thinking by adopting a logic of history that transcends factual reality. In so doing, Rassinier, an exemplary madman, brought to a climax the temptation or, to be more precise, the perversion of the century.

4

In Search of the True Victims, or the Disgrace of the Damned

"This event is unthinkable; therefore it did not occur." So say the metaphysicians of history when they talk about the extermination of the Jews in the gas chambers. And miraculously they are not exactly preaching in the desert, for here and there a few people lend an ear and welcome their "revelations." To what do they owe this newly found, affectionate curiosity? As they themselves freely admit, they owe it to Israel or, more specifically, to the growing disfavor and gradual degradation that the image of Israel has suffered in public opinion: "Up until and throughout the Six-Day War, French public opinion was imbued with a sort of transfer Zionism: corresponding to the crime of Auschwitz was a de facto reparation, namely the existence of a mythically peacemaking, socializing Israel. The Palestinian question's rapid advance to the forefront—and especially the absolute, categorical refusal by Israelis and Zionists to consider even looking for a solution to the displacement of populations that they had instigated—served to reveal a different reality."[1]

Formerly, Israel was untouchable because of the proximity of the genocide. Today the genocide is subject to dispute due to alleged behavior by Israel. Two distinct sorts of resentment come together and join forces in the negation of the gas chambers: acrimony over an atypical fact, and irritation caused by the prestige and impunity that this barbarity confers upon its victims and their descendants. Metaphysical motives (putting some sense into the evolving course of events) combine with the political temptation to refashion history in light of current events and project the stakes of present-day reality into the past. It is the originality of the phenomenon in the first case and its supposed beneficiaries in the second that lead thinking down the path of revision. The contestation of a privilege, the rejection of what is concealed from the light of history, of what stands out in strong contrast with all logic, all anticipation: the inalterable serenity of orthodox thinkers encounters the mounting hatred for Israel, and this convergence instills a formidable vigor into the work of the negation.

THE POLITICS OF GENOCIDE

Millions of people died *in a total loss*, for nothing. We know (in the best of cases) how to become indignant at the enormity of the massacre; we do not know how to comprehend it. A whole people was destroyed, a collectivity disappeared, and there is no compensation, nor any remedy, for this permanent impoverishment of human diversity. "The Germans robbed history of one of its orientations. Genocide is the most odious of crimes, for it inflects the future and reduces certain nourishing roots to shreds" (George Steiner).

If we thought the genocide through instead of simply regretting it, we would be led to put a minus sign on the time in which we are living. We would know that the present is lacking, that it is not something improved but something left over, that it is reached by elimination, through the subtraction of all other virtualities of history, and not, as our celebratory perception of historical evolution would have it, by the pure and simple addition of previous eras. Which means that the present is a *possibility that was lucky enough to come to be*. Which also means that the course of things would have been changed if some men who were not born and who will never be born had been lucky enough to be born. How can we think this, or more especially, how can we feel this? We do not have the faculty to do so. Whether or not we are followers of a logic of history, we pride ourselves on living in a necessary time. Pride? The word is excessive, for we do not even make a claim to this necessity; it constitutes the prereflective evidence enveloping us. It therefore seems normal to us that the Jews did not die in vain. The opposite—which in this case is the truth—would be inconceivable. Thus we spontaneously mitigate the genocide by looking for a meaning to its absurdity and entertaining the notion that such an affront is reparable. Israel, for the Zionists, is that meaning and that reparation. The slogan "Never again" justifies the Hebrew State, and in return, the existence of Israel gives a minimal justification to the genocide.

But as we know, more than thirty years after independence, the establishment of the Jews in Palestine still has irreducible enemies whose numbers continue to grow. And this hostility is turning Hitler's crime into the stakes of a merciless battle. Preyed upon by political language, the genocide can no longer be sheltered from the meaning with which partisans and opponents of Zionism invest it. The outrage committed against the Jewish people is a useful *argument* for some, while for those on the opposing side it is an *inconvenience*, an ideological handicap that must be compensated for or altogether eliminated. Traditionally they do this in two modes of argumentation. First of all, Arabs are not responsible for the setting, the authors, or the victims of what was a European massacre. Why would the West restore its good conscience by proxy? You do not repair one injustice by committing another against an innocent people. Secondly, Auschwitz did not give unlimited credit to its survivors and their descendants. The Israelis cannot drape themselves in their past victimization since they themselves have become executioners in their efforts to establish and consolidate their State.

We must take pause here and consider the profound meaning of such argumentation. It has long been known that demagogy is part of the requisite arsenal of all power (and all opposition). We are well acquainted with the tricks of our political orators, their tactics of seduction, and their agreeable or exalted efforts not to appear as though they are trying to fool anyone. What is perhaps not so well known is that there is no conflict of interest or power that is not also first and foremost a *battle for denomination*. The outcome of struggles depends on the name given to things: to dictate law is to impose one's vocabulary, and conversely, to impose one's vocabulary on public opinion is to take an option on victory, regardless of any momentary weakness. This explains why it is no coincidence that ever since the State of Israel was created, anti-Zionism has been conducting a relentless battle for the Judaization of its cause and the appropriation of impressive key words. In the midst of military and political confrontation, another guerrilla war unfolds: an imperceptible but major offensive, a rhetorical combat in which it is a matter of transferring onto the Palestinians the terms most heavily laden with Nazi-era horror. Zionism is assimilated with a form of *racism* within "the very center of Western intellectual and political culture."[2] Its guiding principle is the Aryan contempt for races and cultures said to be inferior; its exclusive goal is territorial expansion. As for the idea of a "Jewish race" so commonplace at the turn of the century, it "is not solely an outgrowth of the millennial persecution of the Jews in Christian Europe but also of the racial typologies of Gobineau, Stewart, Chamberlain, and Renan."[3] There is no need to insist on this point, as the role of the first two authors in the formation of Hitler's doctrine is widely recognized. For those who want everything spelled out, let us be even more explicit: "Our world is now confronted with the emergence of a new type of Nazism whose followers proclaim that their doctrine goes far back in history."[4]

And daily politics only confirms this in-depth diagnosis of the thinking that led to the creation of the State of Israel. A steady stream of propaganda has familiarized us with the idea that there are two hotbeds of evildoing on the globe, two great stains of infamy: South Africa and the "Zionist entity." Because of apartheid in the one country and in spite of a parliamentary regime bordering on ungovernability in the other, the epithet of *fascist* is applied to these two countries in the most natural, straightforward manner. Finally the occupation of the West Bank is purged of its specific intent and is absorbed part and parcel in the Occupation (with a capital *O*), which obviously is to say the German occupation during the dark years of World War II. This one hypnotic word abolishes the reality it designates and substitutes in its place the trauma of Oradour, the torture of Jean Moulin, and the image of searches carried out in the pale light of dawn by Gestapo agents in leather coats. The dead takes hold of the living: a single name turns history into poetry's prey and throws the protagonists into the prescripted roles of ss and resister. In this way the Israeli-Palestinian conflict gets caught in the mechanics of resurrection and disguise, a situation that puts it on the same level with the great Hitlerian tragedy. What do the characteristics of the Israeli occupation matter, and of what importance are its daring moves and its retreats, its oscillations between repressive and liberal phases? The name with which it is baptized converts the present into the past and history into pure mythology. Events are doomed to mimicry; the opposing actors merely lend their bodies to ghosts: the world puts on a play that has already been staged before, except that this time a change in casting has taken place. While the plot is the same, the Jews no longer play the part of the hero; this time they are cast as the engineers of disaster, and that is what is new in this revival. The drama of the Middle East thus transcends its own time and is played out *in costume*. The Palestinian cause takes on the prestige of both the Resistance (since it is fighting against the Occupation) and the yellow star (since the Palestinians are the Jews of Israel), whereas the Hebrew State, in all its arrogance and fierceness, resuscitates that absolute evil, Nazism.[5]

And as might be expected, the word "genocide" is the object of particular avidity and fervor. To gain possession of this decisive term is to win the lexical battle, which frees up the potential for all other triumphs. Hence the importance of the notion of "moral genocide" in anti-Zionist writings.

When a people like the Palestinians is not recognized as existing, when it is refused its homeland, its national existence and identity, as well as the fundamental rights and freedoms given to other peoples, what is left of it, what is left for it? It becomes a "nonpeople": the individuals of whom it is composed become "nonpersons." Is this not in fact a genocide, a moral genocide?[6]

Thanks to the Israeli aircraft's bombing of the Palestinian headquarters in Beirut in July 1981, moral genocide was able to blossom into genocide proper, into physical liquidation of the Palestinian people. The public's anger and stupor over the raid's devastating toll of nearly four hundred deaths are still with us. So is the first term used to express that indignation: genocide. Whether out of scruples or respect for what they remembered, some people hesitated to use the word, but they were even more reticent to criticize its use, for fear of weakening the condemnation or even of being accused of spinelessness, of guilty sympathy for the aggressors. The feeling of revolt was considered too well-justified to be attacked on the grounds of its language. The word was "accepted" as appropriate because of the horror of the event.

Now what happens when a bombing is described in terms of a final solution? The first crime is exaggerated, the second one is minimized, and so two lies are told. With the first crime, it is the murderous action that takes on the character of the exceptional; but after that, it is the very idea of genocide that is trivialized, loses its own reality, and can be used to describe any and all infamous military actions, making no distinctions among them. There is some previsionism in this *verbal incontinence*. Used in contexts to which it does not apply, weakened by its metaphorical use, and degraded by needless repetition, the term "genocide" is wearing out and dying. This *exhaustion of meaning* makes it easier for the workers for the negation to do their job. If all brutality accedes to the name of genocide, then Jewish persistence is absolutely unintelligible. Peremptory in the manner in which they recall the past, the "Zionists" assert that their catastrophe is unique and that it must be protected against the relentless desire to trivialize it, whether that desire is expressed overtly or in an underhanded manner. What evidence do they provide to support their claim? As they would have it, theirs was the most merciless genocide, the most efficient and most scientific of all genocides. But does the word "genocide" not mean massacre, and do current events not present us with their share of bloody military operations? Conclusion: it is a dog-eat-dog world, and Jews cannot exploit genocide as their own particular destiny or as something specific to their history. In the final analysis, what they are hiding behind their fight against oblivion is the far less glorious desire to have the lion's share. Why? To put it simply, in order to have unlimited rights. To sanction their arrogance and to legitimate the injustices and acts of violence perpetrated since 1948 by the Hebrew State, in the name of the supposedly incomparable agony suffered by Jews.

As time passes, it is hard to resist taking this line of reasoning a step farther. Given their ability to *repeat* on other people the treatment that they themselves experienced, the Zionists could go so far as to *misrepresent* the suffering of their people, if only to sidetrack public opinion and prolong their status as victims well beyond its legitimate time frame. It is therefore only natural that certain anti-Zionists got carried away in their fervor and went from genocide as a metaphor for Israeli oppression, to negation, or to a mitigating revision of the Nazi genocide. Of course the somber days of Nazism are still part of our living memory, and many who hate "the Zionist entity" draw the line at this type of mental shift. In taking Faurisson's side Vincent Monteil remains an impassioned exception within the bosom of anti-Zionism. Nevertheless there still exists the tendency to try to *rewrite Jewish history in function of the antipathy inspired by Israel*. And the future belongs to this burgeoning proclivity. Hampered these days by the vigilance of survivors, it will have less and less trouble making itself heard as the Nazi trauma is erased and the superego of living memory fades away. After reading the present in light of the recent past and condemning Israel for committing all of Hitler's sins, one (that is to say, anyone subscribing to anti-Zionism in its most radical form) will gradually get used to doing the opposite: one will henceforth look at a historical past only to see the Zionists' preparatory maneuvers for the edification of Israel, with the West's money *and* guilt. Or in keeping with a more sophisticated version of the negation that distorts everything without disturbing anything, one will superimpose today's image of the Jews on the Jews of yesterday, and one will say that jealous of their prerogatives and intoxicated with their own genius, they expiated their sin of pride in the extermination. The disaster of days gone by will be the harbinger of the coming apocalypse. One will project into that distant past the future punishment looming on the Zionist horizon.

Such is Israel, a superior state, having every right and no duty, enjoying a permanent impunity, proud and absolute, modern in the exercise of death, ancient in its dialectic that sooner or later will lead it to new dispersions, that is to say, to a supreme apocalypse, like a great tragedy. It will be alone. The sole author of its martyrdom. *Alone against the world, which will have given up understanding the slightest thing about the destiny of a people born to be chosen and dead from having been so.*[7]

Tahar Ben Jelloun, who sees where history is leading, is ahead of his time. He is setting a date, and in less than a generation, his notions about Israel will be widespread. For him, the Israeli government's present intolerance, the past sorrows of the Jewish people, and the inevitable extinction of the Hebrew State are the effects of one and the same cause: election. Israel is guilty of the death to which it is destined, just as the Jews in the camps of Poland fulfilled their destiny of absolute solitude. Examined in the hindsight of those who hate Israel, Jewish history will soon vacillate between two categories: the Lie (you are blowing your suffering out of proportion) and Punishment (you have only yourselves to blame for your terrible suffering, both that which occurred in the past and that which the future holds in store for you).[8]

BIOGRAPHY OF A NEOLOGISM

The word is not yet forty years old. It was coined in 1944. At the height of the war. "New ideas require new words." While studying the Nazi administration in occupied Europe,

In Search of the True Victims

Raphaël Lemkin, a Polish lawyer and Jew who had emigrated to the U.S., forged this bastardized term from the Greek *genos* ("race," "tribe") and the Latin root *cide* ("murder"). He thereby introduced for national, ethnic, or religious groups the concept of what homicide is for the individual: the rejection of the right to existence.

In its most general sense, genocide does not necessarily signify the immediate annihilation of a nation, except in the case where it is carried out through the direct massacre of all its members. The word designates a methodical, coordinated plan that aims to destroy the foundations of life of national groups, the ultimate design being the annihilation of the groups themselves.

Genocide is directed against the national group as such, and the actions it implies are directed against individuals, not in their standing as individuals but as members of national groups.[9]

Nazi crimes made it painfully obvious that a gap separated certain modern day practices from international jurisdiction. It was specifically to help fill that gap that Raphaël Lemkin coined the term "genocide." But he had already been toying with the idea for quite some time. As early as the 1930s, he had been denouncing the insufficiencies of the conventions of the Hague. Such conventions dealt only with the rights of individuals and the sovereignty of nation states, with no word on preserving the integrity of peoples. Since World War I and the collapse of the Hapsburg monarchy, there had arisen the problem of *stateless nations* that were called minorities—their status, their security, and their rights in the *nation states* that had just achieved independence. At a conference held in 1933 under the aegis of the League of Nations, Lemkin proposed the statutory recognition of two new crimes: *barbarity*, or destructive action against the members of a national group; and *vandalism*, the destruction of works deemed cultural in that they are the expression of the genius particular to different peoples. But the states were too concerned with their sovereignty to accommodate this demand. Lemkin's proposal was rejected by the conference. It also cost him his job when he returned to Poland (he had been secretary to the Warsaw court of appeals since 1927). In this way he was the guinea pig for his own theses. He was punished for having given the Polish state's anti-Semitism a rigorous definition: barbarity and vandalism.

After the war broke out, Lemkin spent two years in hiding and then succeeded in fleeing to the United States. It was thanks to his personal, unrelenting determination that the United Nations General Assembly adopted a convention for the prevention and repression of the crime of genocide. However, the vote of 9 December 1948 was only a half-measure; since that date, in fact, international legislation has identified a new crime but has not given itself the means to punish it. With no international court having managed to be established, the only possibility of punishment consists of having persons accused of genocide appear before the courts of the state in which the acts were committed. But any project to exterminate entire human groups as such can be conceived, worked out, and executed only by the states themselves. So it is up to the potentially guilty to pass judgment on their own crimes, a circumstance that gives us reason to be skeptical about any such repression of genocide.

But despite its lack of real legal efficacy, the word has made a major impact on everyday language—so major, in fact, that the word may die of overuse. It must be said that for the world that grew out of the ruins of war, there could forever after be only one definition of barbarity. The universal conscience formed itself anew by putting the face of Hitlerism on absolute evil. It is said that 1914 was the death of a civilization. In 1939, civilization in general felt itself being swept away by a monstrous enemy that was all the more disturbing for having been engendered within. Since then, Nazism is invoked almost religiously to represent civilization's Other; and to represent Nazism, one invokes its supreme horror, the physical annihilation of peoples or ethnic groups denied human status.

Thus a confusing give-and-take between the concrete and the incorporeal, between reality and symbol, has come about: the Führer made evil real and at the same time made himself less real through that eternal essence. Satan was incarnated in the person of Hitler, who from then on was merely the allegory of the demon. Nazism, the ultimate truth of oppression and the model for all abominations past and future, also became the reference for all accusatory discourse. The event was seized, taken in, and abstracted by the Idea, and the Idea inevitably deteriorated into insult: if everyone agrees on a single definition of the enemy, everyone is tempted to apply that image to his own opponent in order to justify the battle he is fighting. Since Hitler's time, every villain is a fascist, and every victim wears the yellow star. There is no revolution, no revolt, no struggle, no matter how minor its object, that fails to go rummaging through the past only to end up presenting itself in terms of this particular period of history. For what is antifascism anyway, if not the ecstasy of a dual age, a mixture of vigilance and parody, the combination of a necessary remembering and a laughable disguise? "The resurrection of the dead, in these revolutions, therefore served to glorify new struggles" (Marx). And shamelessly the genocide was incorporated into this effort to dramatize things. It was the poetry of our prose, the passion in its confrontations, the conversion of the ordinary world into a tragic one, the inspiration needed to allow militants to rise above day to day ambitiousness. Every oppressed minority from women to Occitanians[10] saw fit to declare *its* genocide, as if *doing anything short of this* would render that minority uninteresting, incapable of being recognized; as if the revindication of genocide were the cornerstone of the justice of the minority's cause and the validity of its aspirations. By using the word invented in 1944 to designate the *putting to death* of entire peoples, today's minority groups affirm their identity and legitimate their existence.

DESTITUTION

Antifascist phraseology has met with universal success. Almost all political enterprises derive their references and vocabulary from the Second World War and bring back into play the dead heroes of those execrable times. It would therefore be fundamentally unfair to denounce the practice as a specifically anti-Zionist transgression. Shrouding history in mythology is undoubtedly unfair, as is skipping over the facts and going straight to the archetypes of the Occupation and the Resistance, but in the aftermath of Hitler, this manner of proceeding is widespread.

Anti-Zionism's specific contribution does not therefore reside in the affirmation that "the Palestinians are the Jews of the Middle East" but in the corollary that "the Jews are not Jewish anymore, they have betrayed their Idea, they have deserted their Model. And they must be penalized for this renunciation."

Antifascism had established the Jew as a *value*: as the gold standard of oppression, as the paradigm of the victim. With anti-Zionism this unit of measure is used against the people who gave it its name. The children of Israel are no longer blamed for being Jewish but for failing to be properly Jewish, fully Jewish. And during the past several years, this criticism has slowly but surely been extended to Jewish behavior in general instead of remaining focused on the problem of

Israel. The blame stretches beyond the bounds (loose as they are) of anti-Zionism, and Judaism as a whole is being accused of arrogance. By whom? This exasperating phenomenon is not easy to pinpoint. No one ideological family has a monopoly on it. With no particular ties and with no ideological home to call its own, it wanders throughout society in defiance of the sacrosanct divisions between the right and the left. Like its counterpoint, it is connected to the decline of anti-Semitism in contemporary France. Its discourse might be summed up as follows: "The Jews are complaining; that is all we hear from them. But *they have the upper hand* and drown out the quiet suffering of the truly oppressed with their deafening clamor. They raise the specter of the pogroms at the drop of a hat, in a country where one can no longer be anti-Semitic. Moaning and groaning they exhale their weakness in heartrending sighs, despite the fact that they have all the major forces working in their favor—the State and its law, society and its conformity, mass media and its hype. The proof: Rue Copernic. A bomb explodes outside a synagogue and there we are, subjected to several weeks of national mourning. It is collective hysteria, an obligatory trance, orchestrated mass sorrow. And woe unto the individualist who refuses to conform to it! He is singled out and condemned as a freethinker.

"France goes into mourning to conjure up an absent threat, and all the while the children of the Sahel go on dying of hunger, and here at home, in the midst of indifference, immigrants, those present-day Jews, are subjected to the effects of ordinary racism.[11] No one ever saw Rothschild being attacked the way immigrants are. In short, the lesson to be learned from the Rue Copernic bombing is that the Jews are profiting from a privileged situation and are public opinion's little darlings, its manipulators even. (You probably noticed that one week after the events of the Rue Copernic, the three major weekly news magazines all had a yellow star on their cover.) And what allows them to turn this powerfulness into vulnerability? The pathos of Auschwitz, the ready obsessional reference to their genocide.

"To go from there to denying the existence of the gas chambers requires making a leap that we will carefully avoid. But all the same, is it not time for the Jewish catastrophe to fall back into line? Copernicus ruffled some feathers and revolutionized thought by showing that the Earth was not the center of the universe. No matter how hurtful and revolutionary it might appear, is it not our task to show that history does not revolve around the Jews? Judeocentrism, that is our weakness and our backwardness—a fact that explains why, subjugated by yesterday's victims, we have been showing such indifference toward the injustices of today. In order to catch up with the times and leave the last war behind, in order to turn the page and finally accede to modernity, Judeocentrism must be eliminated. And long live the revisions that enable us to do so!"

It is true that Faurisson is almost universally repudiated, yet at the same time, there is the increasingly widespread idea that the Jews are no longer Jewish, that they have lost their vocation, and that these defrocked Jews are clinging to their former priesthood with all the means at their disposal, with no thought to the cost. There is a prevailing climate of destitution, as evidenced by the article summarizing the trial that appeared in the newspaper *Le Monde* and whose title, "Members of the University Community Clash over the Faurisson Case," suggests that truth and imposture have equal footing in the academic milieu:

So on the one side are those who fear that the hydra is coming back to life and who do not want to forget the horror of the camps or let an incontestable, immutable history grow dull. On the other side are those who think that the Jewish people do not have a monopoly on suffering, that there is no exemplary torture—the gas chambers—any more barbaric than the rest. They do not deny the sheer scale of Nazi crimes, but they find it excessive to consider them to be the most odious of all. To do so, they say, makes other war crimes, past and present, always seem less serious and ultimately more excusable in comparison.[12]

What a strange way to sum up the opposing theses! In his attempt to balance them, to give them equal respectability, Christian Colombani, the author of the article, defuses "revisionism" to the point of turning a negation into an interpretation of the genocide. If we are to believe the journalist, the erasers are not erasing anything: they are not contesting the existence of the gas chambers; they are simply content to deny it any and all exemplary character. It is not the fact that is eliminated, for everyone seems to be in agreement on the fact; it is only its significance that is inflected and its preeminence that is put into question. Here is Faurisson exculpated of the very crime that landed him in court, as if nothing had happened, in the subdued appearance of pure description (on the one side . . . on the other . . .). The violence of this judgment of reality (this did not take place!) is surreptitiously toned down to a value judgment: this (the genocide) is a relative event, not an absolute one.

Is this dishonesty? Is it blindness? It hardly matters whether the gross distortion is deliberate or unconscious. What counts, what needs to be analyzed, is the impatience, the nervousness that made it possible. In effect the "revisionists" are proven innocent only to be in a better position to impugn their opponents. Deprived of their principal argument—falsification—those who subscribe to an "immutable history" look like new inquisitors. Through their passionate attachment not to the truth but to the exemplariness of the gas chambers, they exhibit a willingness to set the Jews apart and especially to set them on a higher plane, well above history's other victims. As the kings of martyrdom, as those persecuted by divine right, the Jews want to corner the market on compassion, and they desperately cling to an unjustifiable privilege. As the constant, inevitable object of some sort of metaphysics of the elite, the Jews supposedly allow pride to lead them into committing one transgression after another. First they invented the aristocratic notion of the *chosen people*, and now they want to exploit their monopoly on suffering to revel in that new, pathetic, and most delightful pleasure: being the *accursed nation*.

So ends the dialectic of the copy and the model: in the early stage—antifascism—the Jews personify the maximal victim. Then, becoming more middle-class in various diasporas and driving the Palestinians out of Israel with rifles and dynamite, they abandon the image of victim and prove to be unworthy of their destiny. Epilogue: the model itself is destitute; the Jewish genocide falls back into the fold. It is said to be a horror like any other, and ironically, no doubt, one speaks of compliance with history to describe this quashing of the event, this subsumption of difference by equivalence.

But the progression is not strictly linear. Its different moments overlap each other, and the traitors and impostors who are the Jews are reproached all at one time for both *abandoning* and *concocting* their role as victim. For we are living at a turning point in time when the fascist past adorns the present while concurrently the stakes of present-day politics shape our memory of that period. Two mythologies intertwine. In the first, the Jews are condemned in the name of their image; in the second, that image itself is normalized because it clashes with the current situation.

The "revisionists" themselves are not immune to this ambiguity. They use the symbol that they impugn, and the very individuals who are the most unrelenting in stripping the Persecution of Israel of its abusive capital P proclaim elsewhere that "The Jew is Faurisson." The Jew—that is to say, the Accursed One, the Other, the Alien, the Wanderer, the Poor One, the Weakling, the Outcast. A Dreyfusian connotation thus hovers persistently over the scandal. The Faurisson affair is itself in keeping with the Dreyfus affair, but the wind is shifting. The modern-day Boideffres, Pellieuxes, and Merciers belong to the people called the Guardians of the Book, and it is a Gentile on whom they are treading, because by challenging official history, this impertinent character dared to defy them.

The negation thus plays on all sides of the issue. As we have already seen, it is the ideological daughter of leftist anti-Dreyfusism; it takes Guesde's refusal to distinguish between the good and the bad members of the enemy class and adapts it to the catastrophes of the twentieth century. Democracy and fascism are equally valid (or invalid), just as, for the majority of Socialists, the republican principles of Dreyfusard France have no more or no less merit than the contempt for human rights exhibited by the other France, the France of Blood and Soil. Symbolically, the negation situates itself under the patronage of Dreyfus, and its authors are not afraid to claim the prestigious image of the persecuted Jew for themselves.

This explains the large proportion of intellectuals not only from the left but "what's more, of Jewish origin" (as Christian Colombani somewhat gleefully notes) among the puny troops of "revisionism." Claude Karnooh, Jean-Gabriel Cohn-Bendit, Jacob Assous, and Gàbor Tamàs Rittersporn are no doubt adding a chapter to the interminable history of self-hatred.[13] But it is an unpublishable chapter, for these hit men of the negation are not seeking to cleanse themselves of Jewish singularity, which flies in the face of classic *selbsthaas*. They are not ashamed of the difference. What pains them is witnessing its evaporation, seeing their community of origin trade in their marginality for middle-class status, for the honors, the subordination—via Israel—to the prizes of imperialism. These disappointed libertarians see the Jews breaking with their Christlike image: this crucified people has become an impudent, prosperous, *pampered* people whose dominant ideology admits the slightest sudden mood swings and amplifies them. They, the disaffected, remain faithful to the authenticity of Judaism. They want to live in keeping with their time and struggle against contemporary forms of oppression rather than founder in complacency and treat a nation (their own) that has changed its colors and principles as the eternal victim of history. Run over by the bourgeois judicial machine, Faurisson seems more Jewish to them than do their protected and well-to-do coreligionists. As for his thesis, it is seductive because it allows them to hand out equal pieces of the *pie of suffering* instead of selfishly hoarding it all, as official Judaism does in its greedy, egotistical, voracious way.

IN THE NAME OF DIFFERENCE

Traditional anti-Semitism cursed the Jews. It is to their *demalediction* that the revision of history has continually devoted itself. One torture victim can hide another, and we need to exhume the bodies hidden by our society's "Judeocentrism." Judging from the strength of the Jews today, it is high time to take this prerogative away from them and put some new damned people in their place.

This book is our anti-Diary of Anne Frank. At a time when French intellectuals are debating whether extermination by gas

*occurred, it reveals and enlivens a mystification far more sig-
nificant in anti-Nazi hagiography than the one concerning the*
historical corrections *made for the good cause that began with
Nuremburg.*[14]

The book in question, *The Men with the Pink Triangle*,
is the story of the concentration-camp experience of a ho-
mosexual who was deported to Buchenwald. As the deli-
cate passage cited above indicates, its combination preface
and manifesto by Guy Hocquenghem was written for the
French edition of the book with a single overarching purpose in mind: dethroning the Jews, those pseudovictims,
those usurpers, those phony pariahs, and having the true
incumbents of catastrophe appear in their immaculate splen-
dor. *A mystification far more significant*: ah! to think that in
such concise terms. . . .

In one sentence Hocquenghem pulls off the argumen-
tative tour de force of proving Faurisson right (there was
indeed a mystification) and launching the negation on a new
course. What are the gas chambers, that trifle, compared
to the much more serious imposture that took place under
the aegis of antifascism? Jews have been consecrated as the
absolute monarchs of the disaster, and the murder of other
minorities has been passed over in silence. Why? How do we
explain that the Jews and only the Jews have been promoted
to the envied status of exemplary victim? The answer quite
simply is that unlike homosexuals, criminals, or the insane,
the Jews were sure to touch the hearts of the masses and constituted the most presentable, most melodramatic victims of
the massacre that the Allies could offer. Hocquenghem tells
us that unlike those orphans of martyrdom, the Poles and
the Gypsies, the men with the yellow triangle enjoyed the
benefits of an all-powerful patronage, namely that of the
American Jewish community.[15] And so we find ourselves

once again on familiar ground: close to Rassinier, who already saw the Jews as being effective and influential enough to force the peaceful hand of Hitler and throw the world into conflict, despite the accords of Munich; and close to Faurisson, too, who sees the myth of the gas chambers originating in "certain American Zionist milieus around 1942."[16]

From the "revisionists" to Hocquenghem, the phobia is identical. What changes is the perspective. It is no longer a matter of trivializing Nazism but of rehabilitating unknown martyrs. Combining ignorance with immodesty, lacking all knowledge of the camps as well as the minimal sense of decency that finding out about absolute deprivation tends to instill in someone who has never experienced any real suffering, Guy Hocquenghem reintroduces into the deportation universe the leftist division between the System and the Bandits who scorn its rules, between Law and Transgression, between the chilly, narrow, sheeplike Norm and the indomitable Margin. For good measure, two divisions superimpose themselves on one another: the dead and the survivors, "traitors to their comrades whom they abandoned in the mortal blaze"; the eclipsed deportees and the official deportees, those exploiters of the genocide who for forty years have been grabbing all the attention for themselves, thus perpetuating the biggest lie in history.

So what does that make the Jewish survivors? Hypocrites and bastards. Not only have they committed the ignominy of coming out of the camps alive, but they are rewriting history in such a way as to be its heroes. These kapos ("survivor" = "kapo") want to pass themselves off as being just; these authorized voices of deportation mercilessly suppress the dissident ones. Which allows Hocquenghem to make this pointed little remark: "I would not have wanted to live in the barracks where Simone Veil was the kapo." Simone Veil was eighteen years old when she was deported to Ravensbrück and Auschwitz. I know, such precise information tends to take the fun out of it. It contests the literalness of the formula that must be taken figuratively in order to appreciate its subtlety. Veil is a metaphorical kapo, first because she survived and then because after having collected prizes and honors she became a government minister. To get herself out of the camp, she needed the energy to leave someone behind in her place or to have someone else die instead of her.[17] The struggle to live: according to Hocquenghem, such was the real law of the camps, which is covered up and suppressed by the "insipid piety of official deportees." They lived off each other, and the most cannibalistic won. In this reverse Darwinism, it was not the best who survived; it was the worst. Caution! Danger! Beware of former deportees, and do not believe "the old-timers who remember the camps" and whom the world press puts on display at regular intervals. These Tartuffes are hiding contemptible secrets beneath their holy exterior. They are throwing the grandiloquent veil of antifascism over the horrible truth.

This was the case of one of my aunts who went back to her hometown of Lvov after the war. Her things had been confiscated and then dispersed by the Germans. After some searching, my aunt tracked down an armoire of which she was especially fond. A Russian woman now had the article in her possession. My aunt went to the woman's house, and proving that the armoire belonged to her, she asked the woman if she could have it back. The woman refused. With this, my aunt was fed up and said she was going to report the whole matter to the police. To which the response was, "Listen, you Jewess, if you came out of German hands alive, it is because you have something to hide. It is I who will report you to the NKVD."[18] (The Russians were in the process of annexing the town that had been Ukrainian, then Polish, then Austrian—under the name of Lemberg—then Polish again). My aunt left Lvov without recovering the armoire or any other pieces of her furniture. Now that their humanist mask has been "yanked off the *mugs* of those who even today lie to us about the camps," I at last know the true moral of this story.

To get back to Simone Veil—she not only survived; she also achieved success. And what a career! No doubt with the same tenacity she must have used to avoid death by sending others to it in her place, terrible Simone managed to raise herself to the upper limits of power. Aside from the insurmountable handicap that being a woman presented to her, do her haughty manner, her hard features, and her hair austerely fashioned in a bun not give her the physical appearance of a slave warden, which is in fact to say, of a kapo?

There is in Hocquenghem's text a quasi-untenable blunder that consists of deciphering the infinitely complex concentration camp world in terms of the infinitely primitive, neolibertarian categories of Repression, Institution, and Marginality. He admits no essential difference between the despotism of a kapo and the prerogatives of a government minister, since these two authorities derive from the same concept, Power—that immutable, compact, evil entity. And if some deported Jews have managed to attain the highest responsibilities without hiding the number each has tattooed on his (or her) arm, does that not disqualify their claim to martyrdom? In addition, does that not mean that already in the camps they were on the dignitaries' side and not on that of the outlaws?

But beyond this retrospective leftism, Hocquenghem's vehemence for the target chosen goes hand in hand with all the other currents of present-day anti-Semitism. Hatred for the Jews is polarizing around Simone Veil with the same unanimity it did around Léon Blum in former days or, more recently, around Pierre Mendès-France. Why Simone Veil?

Because she is a deportee who has met glory and because she therefore symbolizes, in all her purity, the modern Jewish scandal: the willingness to play on all sides, by being at the same time the Powerful and the Excluded, the Sovereign and the Victim, and even, in the supreme Machiavellian posture, the *one through the other*.

In the nineteenth century, burgeoning nations attained self-awareness through the idea of *election*. Thus Adam Mickiewicz assigned Poland the mission of delivering the masses from their subjugation to the Golden Calf.[19] For his part, Dostoevsky celebrated Russia as the "sole 'theophoric' people, the one people who would renovate and save the universe in the name of a new god, the sole people who held the keys to life and a new word."[20] But an old tribe blocked this self-discovery in the mirror of messianism: the Jewish community—which, long before anyone else, had taken upon itself to claim a spiritual vocation and which, through sheer determination to remain in existence, seemed to deny other nations the opportunity to come together as a chosen people. That spot was already occupied, and it would take some elbowing to oust its Jewish occupant. It was necessary to annihilate—symbolically, at least—that ossified caste hampering the march of history and claiming as its own a privilege it had lost long ago. Already in the high Middle Ages, Christians considered themselves justified in persecuting the Jews because Christians were the *new Israel*.

In making his case for homosexuals, Hocquenghem echoes accents of this *anti-Semitism of rivalry*. Not that he disputes the Jews' metaphysical quality as the *chosen* (our modern minority members scoff at metaphysics). The exasperated jealousy that drives him covets instead the condition, or should I say the rank, of *alien*. He essentially tells the Jews, "You are not the great outcasts of our culture.

In Search of the True Victims

You owe your reputation as the weakest people in history to your skills for intrigue, to your schemes, your influence, your trickery, in other words to your strength in all its forms. Your very power has permanently ensconced you as the stars of misfortune. Your positions as both impresarios and actors have made you the stars of oppression. Obviously you want it all: the identical and the other, integration and ostracism, the prestige of the pariah and the centrality of power. You are acting like spoiled children, and it is time to put an end to your reign: the kingdom of your exile belongs to us, the homosexuals bound up in 'a genocide for which there is not the slightest prospect of reparation.' "[21]

Again recently a certain Jewish idea shaped minority consciousness. Indeed, the oppressed frequently referred to the dignity of the yellow star to affirm the value of their being, in face of the oppressors' scorn. The slave discovered that he was his master's Jew, loved himself in that image, and drew therefrom the energy to proclaim his difference instead of subscribing to the denigration of which he was the object. Hocquenghem inflects this mimetism as hostility. War succeeds imitation. The model you wish to resemble becomes the rival you must supplant in order to feel alive yourself. The metaphorical principle (be like the Jews) leads to the violence of this murderous principle: it's us or them. There is not enough room for two categories of untouchables.

It is probably too late to stem the tide of mythology. It is true that one can confront Hocquenghem with his monumental ignorance. And when he says, for example, that "an unbreakable rule prohibited homosexuals from assuming any job of responsibility in the camps," one can recall, for example, that the *Lagerältest* [camp elder] of Birkenau was for several months a man wearing the pink triangle. Holding this position of camp leader was, of course, unthinkable for a Jew. But is it possible to go beyond counting up individual errors? Will one be understood if one says that, *properly speaking*, there was no genocide of homosexuals? The equivalent of a final solution was not implemented against this minority. In the Europe subject to Nazi occupation, gays were not hunted down with the methodical frenzy and the totalitarian efficiency exercised everywhere against the Jews. They were not forced to wear a star. They were not regrouped into distinct quarters to be condemned to the slow death of the ghettos or to industrial extermination. Homosexuals as a group were not gassed the way Jews and Gypsies were. (I almost forgot, the gas chambers are a fraud established by the Jews in order to ensure the predominance of their own story, to throw other persecuted people down the black hole of history, so that the Jews alone—those crafty devils!— can make off with the tidy sum of money from German reparations and, last of all, put the stamp of approval on the Judeocentric version of the unfortunate events. Once again, it is not to excuse the masters, but rather to defend the interests of unrecognized or suppressed victims that this all too specific form of putting people to death is being challenged.)

What good does it do to argue? No longer is genocide a concept but a title, a mark of respectability and excellence. Anyone who deprives homosexuals of this distinction is doubly contemptible: he is guilty of bigotry and selfishness both at the same time. The Jew inside us censures the suffering of these other outcasts, while the Puritan scorns their desire and collaborates in its interdiction.

Undoubtedly the "revisionists" will fail in their efforts, and future generations will not regard the gas chambers as a hoax. But we should not be too quick to celebrate this probable fiasco. For although it is possible to rescue a given material reality from the obliterative work of the negation, we no longer have any way of fighting against the deviation or the *falsification of words*. It is relatively easy to respond to one discourse with another, but how does one respond to what has ceased to be a personal choice and has become a commonplace—that is, a collective way of speaking? One cannot have a sword fight with vocabulary. That negation is an anonymous one that is confused with what is tending increasingly to be the correct use of words: *without intending any harm* but merely under the effect of a lexical perversion, the monstrous events of the last war "are resituated within the banal course of bygone horrors" (Marthe Robert), since in "Newspeak," as we have seen, genocide is a guarantee of marginality, a certificate of oppression that minority groups award to themselves.[22] Because legitimacy is so closely tied up with genocide, to refuse these groups their claim to genocide is to expose oneself to the ideological infamy of not recognizing their difference. Thanks to this overpowering blackmail, the mythical meaning of the term gradually prevails over its literal meaning. Once this victory is definitive, the past will be lost and the truth will no longer stand a chance.

We must admit, however, that Guy Hocquenghem is not totally without merit. His exaggerated rage will at least have allowed the unnoticed ambiguities of the famous *right to difference* to come to light. This theme normally presents only its sunny side: the willingness to be done with the antiquated, immemorial triumph of identity over alterity; the desire to save the West from its own demons by eradicating its deplorable propensity to accept the foreign only if it is stripped of its particularity and reduced to the role of alter ego, of the other self. A veritable transmutation of values, the right to difference promotes human diversity against the directly totalitarian or deceitfully standardizing will to subjugate men to a single model of behavior. The revindication of this new right denounces two opposite forms of the same allergy: the *intolerance* that punishes heretics or represses deviants and the *tolerance* that requires assimilation as payment in kind. Thus the people of all groups, all ethnicities, all nations, and all perversions seem compelled to join forces in a global battle for emancipation from the great authorities of conformity (the State, the Law, the Norm) who deny them the opportunity to live as they would please.

But being different is not only a new and legitimate right. As Hocquenghem's rage clearly demonstrates, it is also a position that outranks the others, a much sought after transcendence and, in fact, the most enviable of thrones: promoted to the dignity of absolute Slave, I deny any and everybody the possibility of pronouncing himself my Master. An exemplary victim, I am God, and nobody has power over me; no one can put my freedom in check and turn it into a responsible conscience. To whom would I owe any *obligation*? My difference is the perpetual, unpayable debt I present to the universe. It is not my place to welcome the Foreigner—I am, forever after, the Foreigner—I am the one to be welcomed. It is not possible to ask for hospitality and, at the same time, to offer it. Being the Other, I am exempted from making the offering; being out of reach, untouchable, and supreme, I have the privilege of being the only one to speak, with the rest of the world being there only to receive my discourse and make an act of contrition in an auspicious silence. I am the mouth, and they, the others, or rather the Non-Others, are the ears. They listen to my difference. Listen to my difference: therein lies the joy of every marginal group. Being the Other opens the door to the paradise of perpetual autobiography. It gives militant support to the delights of the "I." It legitimates narcissism by rescuing it from gravity, frivolity, and consequently, from remorse. Being the Other is a way of dodging the human relationship the way one dodges the law, a way of substituting a favorable dissymmetry for an exacting reciprocity. By virtue of a right to express oneself, it is a self-liberation from the need to hear.

We said at the outset of this book that facts are not stubborn. "Others" are not stubborn either, if we may say so, and there are two ways of getting rid of them that are also two ways of wiping out the aspect of obligation that exists in the conscience: *in the name of Sameness*, by forcing the unfamiliar individual to squelch his difference; *in the name of the Other*, by dwelling in transcendence or exteriority oneself, and on a permanent basis.

The first of these devices holds no secrets for the Jews: being used to its rhetoric, its violence, and its traps, they know how to denounce it, if not always how to fight against it effectively. Instead of playing the assimilation game and excusing themselves for being different, they now are ready to defend and to "assume" their difference. But perhaps they (we) are only following in the enemy's footsteps. In fact it is likely that in abandoning the language of sameness, future anti-Semitism *will rely on difference* in order to spew its diatribes and will tap the untainted prestige of alterity for its energy and its new innocence.

Epilogue
Prejudice and Paradox

To exclude the Jews just really will not do; to exterminate them is not enough: we should also cut them out of history, remove them from the books through which they speak to us, blank out at last that presence that, prior to and in the wake of any book, the inscribed word constitutes, a presence through which man, from the most distant, horizonless reaches, has already turned toward man—in short, eliminate "others." Maurice Blanchot

Vigilance is necessary. We have to go over the past in order to avoid its coming back to haunt us. But vigilance is also a delusion that gives the look of the most recent past to the near future. Drawing the lessons of immediate history, vigilance condemns evil to resurfacing tomorrow in yesterday's guise. As we proclaim "No more Hitler" and identify hatred toward Jews with militant fascism, we make ourselves blind to the nonfascist forms that anti-Semitism can assume. We are tricked by our own attention to the matter: blindness and clear-sightedness go hand in hand in this insomnia of memory. Hence the two overriding attitudes in the gas chambers affair: either one has unthinkingly and with no proof accused the authors of the negation of being neo-Nazis; or, when that hypothesis crumbled, one became receptive to their argumentation, thinking that since these are not fascists speaking, they must have a point. In short, only the racism of the masters is intolerable, only elitist prejudice, the flaunted repulsion for "inferior beings." But when expressed in the form of revolt or complaint, this very same hatred provokes the opposite reaction. The effect of a word depends not on its content but on who enunciates it. In the mouth of an oppressed person, or of someone speaking on behalf of the oppressed, a racist statement becomes a legitimate revindication or even a revolutionary act. The ruthless critique of those in power is accompanied by an unlimited indulgence toward all discourse bearing the stamp of resistance or, quite simply, of suffering.

But Nazi racism is perhaps only an enigmatic, exceptional moment in the long history of anti-Semitism: for the first time, the masters acknowledged that they were the masters, and their ideology explicitly glorified one racial group's superiority over all others. The torturers were leaders; the Jews were lowly worms. Previously the persecutors of Jews had considered themselves the victims of Jews or at least the avengers of Him whom the Jews had crucified.

Now, even with today's secularized version of it, we rely heavily on a Christian vision of history. The suffering underclasses and humiliated peoples of the world remain reincarnations of the God-made-man. The Jews have unconsciously been Christianized by antifascism. Reduced to a state of destitution verging on animality, and being the victims of infinite degradation, they have followed in the Savior's footsteps, retracing the path of the Stations of the Cross. It is the irony of fate that the Jews became likable when they became the Christ figure. It was a formidable misunderstanding that made them popular (sometimes even in their own eyes). People praised in the Jews an image that contradicted the very message of Judaism. They were good because they were victims, whereas Judaism rejects such sentimental confusion of suffering with justice, a confusion implied by the enhancement of the victim as such. "Suffering has no magical effect. The just man who suffers is worthy not because of his suffering, but because of his justice, which defies suffering."[1]

Epilogue

It would certainly seem that the Jews are now poised to be decrucified, and the revision of the genocide is one of many signs of this. Other *passions* are appearing on the scene, along with other agonies more topical and more urgent, and the people of Auschwitz are being deposed in favor of these recent victims. Then too, the State of Israel is precipitating this disgrace by aggravating it: in a fatal symmetry those who formerly awaited execution are becoming in turn the executioners, and our Christian vision of history is turning against the Jews (after having doted on them for all of one instant in history) and is *unwittingly* renewing age-old imprecations against them.[2]

Such is the strangeness of the world in which we live: anti-Semitic prejudice is regressing and fading away—as evidenced by the impressive reaction of solidarity in the wake of the bombing on the Rue Copernic—at the same time that the Jews are resuming their ancient role as a dominating people who feel sure of themselves. Geopolitics is restoring to them that diabolical stature that they are losing in everyday life. Daily discourse is normalizing them; historical discourse (or at least one of its most widespread versions) is demonizing them. At one time or another, these two evolutions will suffer a clash, and no one can as yet predict what form it will take.

There remains this disturbing certainty: no matter how much one would like to think so, anti-Semitism cannot be reduced to a set piece of nonsense, to a generally accepted idea; it is not an allergy planted in the child's mind by preceding generations, an inert way of thinking that passes from mouth to mouth and brain to brain. The hatred toward Israel (in the large sense) must not be confined to the category of *prejudice*. Sometimes prejudice acts as a vehicle for hatred and sometimes, as is the case today, as a foil.

Epilogue

Protected by the armor plating of his taboos, conventional middle-class man exalts similarity, blocks all routes of escape from it, and imagines only a homogeneous world where he lives out his life in the comfort, and the dullness, of identity. The fascist (and, in this case, the thinker on the new right) drowns in his dreams of hierarchy and, in opposition to egalitarian decadence, magnifies the gulf that separates the weak from the strong.

Rejection of the Other and contempt for the Humble Man: these two racist reflexes are being fought by those who are reinventing anti-Semitism today. For they are speaking out against sameness in favor of the other, in favor of the victim and against the powerful.

We are living in the constant chimera of rupture and novelty; we think of ourselves as unyieldingly modern. But the idea that a declaration of newness is all that it takes to extinguish the activity of old entities is one of the great illusions of our time. Just the opposite is true: continuity is never possible or acceptable except when it is disguised as rupture. By changing its style, by moving away from prejudice to paradox, from the dominant ideology to the defense of the dominated, anti-Semitism is being reproduced *without being transmitted*. Thus in all good conscience, and with full consciousness of all things new, the hackneyed theme of Jewish arrogance is being reborn. Moreover we are living the historic moment when this idea is acquiring enough strength to become *retroactive*: how can a people so powerful today have been so weak before? Or this more sophisticated variant of the same question: has this nation not (re)built its strength on the exploitation of its misfortunes and on the selfish, exploitative confiscation of all the pity the world has to offer? Undoubtedly the story of the gas chambers will not be erased from the record of human events. Truth will prevail over the negation. But this material victory will not end the revision of the Jewish genocide, nor will it stop muzzled differences or unrecognized victims from indicting those who supposedly assumed the monopoly on suffering in order to establish their hegemony. Indeed as these two attitudes advance, they are following in history's direction.

Notes

1. The term "negationism" was coined by Henry Rousso in *The Vichy Syndrome* (Cambridge: Harvard University Press, 1991) to distinguish between "revisionism," which, as Rousso argues, usually refers to "a normal phase in the evolution of historical scholarship," and the denial of the Holocaust, where "what is at issue is a system of thought, an ideology, and not a scientific or even critical approach to the subject" (151). More recently, in the context of the Garaudy–Father Pierre affair, Robert Redeker has argued that, although some in France still insist on a distinction between the two terms in discussing the Holocaust, the differentiation is a false one and only serves the purposes of the deniers. Redeker argues that the end pursued in both cases is the same, the only difference being that "negationism moves directly toward its goal" whereas revisionism adopts a more subtle strategy of minimization rather than outright denial. See Robert Redeker, "La toile d'arraignée du révisionnisme," *Les Temps Modernes* 589 (August–September 1996): 1.

2. According to Pierre-André Taguieff, Pierre Guillaume announced the publication of Garaudy's book to members of the press in November 1995 and sent a similar announcement to the "Friends of La Vieille Taupe" on 15 December. See Pierre-André Taguieff, "L'abbé Pierre et Roger Garaudy. Négationnisme, antijudaïsme, antisionisme," *Esprit* 8–9 (1996): 210. The edition of the book for sale to the general public was published at Garaudy's expense. On the cover and on the binding, Garaudy lists the publisher as "Samizdat Garaudy." The use of the word "Samizdat" clearly suggests an effort to draw a comparison between Garaudy's book and those "self-published"—"samizdat"—works by East European dissidents protesting communist oppression. All page references in the text are to this edition.

3. Denunciations of Israeli and American racism have of course regularly been part and parcel of "negationism" in France, especially since Noam Chomsky's defense of Robert Faurisson, an episode to which we shall return. But earlier "negationist" texts by Faurisson and Paul Rassinier concern themselves primarily with the details of what might be called the denial itself: contesting testimony by witnesses and victims, alternative explanations for the uses of the gas chambers, etc.

4. The strategy of conflating Nazi crimes with those committed by "whites"—Americans, Europeans, and Israelis—against people of color in the Third World and former colonies was also, of course, used by Jacques Vergès in his defense of Klaus Barbie in the mid–1980s. For a discussion of the trial and Vergès's strategy, see Alain Finkielkraut, *Remembering in Vain: The Klaus Barbie Trial and Crimes against Humanity*, trans. Roxanne Lapidus, with Sima Godfrey (New York: Columbia University Press, 1992).

5. See Taguieff, "L'abbé Pierre et Roger Garaudy," 210.

6. See Simone Veil, "Ils ont profité de nos erreurs," *L'Evénement du jeudi*, 27 June–3 July 1996, 22. The Gayssot Law was passed in the wake of the desecration of a Jewish cemetery in the southern town of Carpentras in May 1990. The desecration produced a wave of national indignation, including massive demonstrations in Paris and elsewhere. Despite the good intentions that prompted its passage, the Gayssot Law has been severely criticized from the beginning. In 1991 Tzvetan Todorov insisted that the criminalization of tendentious interpretations of history was "grotesque" and went on to say: "Truth does not need a law in order to be protected; if law becomes necessary, it's because the legislator has doubts about it being the truth." See Tzvetan Todorov, "Letter from Paris: Racism," *Salmagundi* 88–89 (fall 1990–winter 1991): 49.

7. See Redeker, "La Toile d'arraignée," 3.

8. The details of Father Pierre's biography as described here are taken from Eric Conan and Sylviane Stein, "Ce qui a fait chuter l'abbé Pierre," *L'Express*, 2–8 May 1996, 20–25.

9. Founded after the Liberation under the leadership of the Resistance leader Maurice Schumann, the MRP was liberal and impec-

cably *résistant*, but it attracted many conservative votes among former Pétainists because of its Catholic affiliation and because no true right-wing party existed at the time in French politics.

10. Father Pierre's comments discussed here are included in a pamphlet published in June 1996 entitled *Le Secret de l'abbé Pierre* (Paris: Editions Mille et une nuits). The authors, Michel-Antoine Burnier and Cécile Romane, were present at discussions between Father Pierre and Bernard Kouchner that were published in book form as *Dieu et les hommes* in 1993. I would like to thank my colleague Nathan Bracher for calling my attention to *Le Secret de l'abbé Pierre*.

11. Father Pierre's comments in *Présent* are quoted in Taguieff, "L'abbé Pierre et Roger Garaudy," 211.

12. In their essay in *L'Express*, Conan and Stein note that Father Pierre backed away from his support of Garaudy when LICRA threatened to remove him from its honorary board.

13. A poll conducted at the height of the controversy indicated that sixty-four percent of Frenchmen had not changed their opinion of Father Pierre as a result of his support of Garaudy. Twenty-four percent were less sympathetic to Father Pierre after the incident, whereas nine percent were now more sympathetic than they had been.

14. See the interview with Gilles Perrault in "La Victoire des révisionnistes," *L'Evénement du jeudi*, 27 June–3 July 1996, 18–19.

15. Along these lines, see Redeker, "La Toile d'arraignée," 1.

16. See Alain Finkielkraut, "Le Siècle de la négation," *L'Evénement du jeudi* 27 June–3 July 1996, 24. Taguieff's term "conspirationalist judeophobia" ("L'abbé Pierre et Roger Garaudy," 211) implies a fear of a worldwide Jewish—or, in its modern garb, Israeli-American—conspiracy for domination and control.

17. Pierre Vidal-Naquet, quoted in Claude Askolovitch, Philippe Cohen, and Vanina Maestracci, "La Victoire des révisionnistes," *L'Evénement du jeudi*, 27 June–3 July 1996, 16.

18. Redeker, "La Toile d'arraignée," 2.

19. See Finkielkraut, "Le Siècle de la négation," 24.

20. Along this lines, see Charles Maier, *The Unmasterable Past: History, the Holocaust, and German National Identity* (Cambridge: Harvard University Press, 1988), esp. 1–34.

21. The claims made by Bardèche in *Nuremberg ou la Terre Promise* are enumerated in Gill Seidel, *The Holocaust Denial: Antisemitism, Racism, and the New Right* (Leeds: Beyond the Pale Collective, 1986), 95.

22. The details provided here concerning Rassinier's life and career are taken from Florent Brayard's excellent recent study of Rassinier and negationism in France, *Comment l'idée vint à M. Rassinier* (Paris: Fayard, 1996).

23. Pierre Vidal-Naquet, "Paul Rassinier ou la dérive retardée," preface to *Comment l'idée vint à M. Rassinier*, by Florent Brayard (Paris: Fayard, 1996), 9–16.

24. See Robert Faurisson, *Mémoire en défense: Contre ceux qui m'accusent de falsifier l'histoire* (Paris: La Vieille Taupe, 1980).

25. Faurisson's comments are included in François Brigneau, *Mais qui est donc le professeur Faurisson? Une enquête, un portrait, une analyse* (Paris: François Brigneau, 1992). They are also cited in Brayard, *Comment l'idée vint à M. Rassinier*, 419–22. It is worthy of note that Brigneau is a former collaborator and currently a right-wing activist who has written for such extremist reviews as *Le Choc du mois*, recently defunct.

26. A detailed discussion of the critical reception of Faurisson's article on Rimbaud's poem can be found in Brayard, *Comment l'idée vint à M. Rassinier*, 422–27.

27. Faurisson, quoted in *Comment l'idée vint à M. Rassinier*, 430.

28. Faurisson, quoted in *Comment l'idée vint à M. Rassinier*, 434.

29. See Nadine Fresco, "Les Redresseurs de morts," *Les Temps Modernes* 407 (June 1980): 2154.

30. Pierre Vidal-Naquet, *Assassins of Memory: Essays on the Denial of the Holocaust*, trans. Jeffrey Mehlman (New York: Columbia University Press, 1992), 21–23.

31. Faurisson had been forced to leave his post at the University of Lyon II because the university administration could no longer guarantee his safety. He had also been assaulted near his home in Vichy.

32. The petition is quoted in its entirety in Serge Thion, ed., *Vérité historique ou vérité politique?* (Paris: La Vieille Taupe, 1980), 163.

33. For discussions and critiques of Chomsky's preface and his role in

the Faurisson affair, see esp. Seidel, *The Holocaust Denial*, 102–4, and Vidal-Naquet, *Assassins of Memory*, 65–73.

34. For a discussion of the charges brought against Faurisson, see Seidel, *The Holocaust Denial*, 106–7.

35. For a discussion of the Touvier affair and its legal complications, see Richard J. Golsan, ed., *Memory, the Holocaust, and French Justice: The Bousquet and Touvier Affairs* (Hanover NH: University Press of New England, 1996).

36. Vidal-Naquet, *Assassins of Memory*, xxiv.

37. Charles Korman, quoted in "La Victoire des révisionnistes," 23.

38. See Seidel, *The Holocaust Denial*, 110.

39. Taguieff, "L'abbé Pierre et Roger Garaudy," 216.

40. For Finkielkraut's background and education, see esp. Judith Friedlander, *Vilna on the Seine: Jewish Intellectuals in France since 1968* (New Haven: Yale University Press, 1990), 92–106.

41. Finkielkraut, "Le Siècle de la négation," 24.

1. THE WORKER, MARTYR, AND SAVIOR

1. For a discussion of the emergence of the new right in France in the 1970s and 1980s and its links to negationism, see Pierre-André Taguieff, "La Nouvelle Judéophobie: antisionisme, antiracisme, anti-impérialisme," *Les Temps Modernes* 520 (November 1989): 1–80. —Introducer

2. Which in no way prevents the adherents of a new "Dark Order" from participating in the elaboration and the diffusion of the hoax. See the investigation by Pierre-André Taguieff, "L'héritage nazi," *Les Nouveaux Cahiers* 64 (spring 1981).

3. Maurice Bardèche, brother-in-law of the martyred fascist writer Robert Brasillach, was the founder of the postwar fascist review *Défense de l'Occident* and author of *Nuremberg ou la Terre promise* (1948), a work that, before Rassinier and Faurisson, championed many of the theses of negationism. Like Faurisson, Bardèche was a professor of literature by profession. Marc Frederiksen was leader of the neofascist FANE (Fédération d'Action Nationale et Européenne), which claimed responsibility for the bomb blast in front of the synagogue on the Rue Copernic in October 1980

(actual responsibility for the bombing was never definitively established). The FANE was dissolved by governmental decree and reconstituted as the FNE (Faisceaux Nationaux et Européens). The group also claims to have provided security at meetings of Jean-Marie Le Pen's Front National. —Intro.

4. Taguieff, "L'héritage nazi," 20.

5. Guesdists, named after Jules Guesde, stressed the importance of the international organization and cooperation of socialist movements. They also opposed compromise with parliamentary democracy in France. The Blanquists, representative of the more radical elements of French socialism, were named after the legendary nineteenth-century revolutionary Auguste Blanqui. Blanqui, who participated in the revolutions of 1830, 1848, and 1871, spent more than half his life in prison for his revolutionary activities. "Possibilism," another strand of nineteenth-century French socialism championed by Paul Brousse and inspired by the moderate ideas of Benoît Mallon, stressed a more conciliatory attitude towards the system and the notion that socialists should strive for reforms that were immediately possible. —Intro.

6. Fernand Pelloutier, *Le Congrès général du parti socialiste français* (Paris: Stock, 1900).

7. Pelloutier, *Le Congrès général*.

8. Jules Guesde, in *Les deux méthodes*, a lecture by Jean Jaurès and Jules Guesde in Lille, 1900 (Paris: Editions Spartacus, 1900), 33.

9. Bernard Lazare was one of Dreyfus's earliest and staunchest defenders. Fernand Pelloutier, a leader of nineteenth-century French anarchism was, according to Richard Sohn, instrumental in shifting anarchism "from the tactics of terrorism and insurrection to labor organizing and confrontational strikes." See Richard Sohn, *Anarchism and Cultural Politics in Fin de Siècle France* (Lincoln: University of Nebraska Press, 1989), 26. —Intro.

10. Jacques Julliard, *Fernand Pelloutier et les Origines du syndicalisme d'action directe* (Paris: Editions du Seuil, 1971), 498.

11. The left/right split did not originate with the Dreyfus affair. That event merely gave it a particular tone, one that persists today. Consider, for example, the bombing on the Rue Copernic, which everyone now agrees was a factor in Giscard d'Estaing's defeat in the 1981 presidential election. The right was not, of course,

implicated in the bombing, but the immediate consequence of missteps and silence on the part of officials was to resuscitate the Dreyfusard left—a fact proving that the affair is still alive and well in contemporary politics.

12. Leszek Kolakowski, *L'Esprit révolutionnaire, suivi de Marxisme, utopie et anti-utopie* (Brussels: Editions Complexe, 1978), 22.

13. Jean Jaurès, "Le manifeste communiste de Marx et Engels," in *Commentaire, Contoverses et Discours* (Paris: Editions Spartacus, 1968), 23.

14. Jean Jaurès, *La Petite République*, 7 September 1901.

15. Charles Péguy, *Morceaux choisis* (Paris: Gallimard), 19. Of all of Jaurès's fellow Socialists at the time of the Dreyfus affair, it was Péguy who went beyond the nobleness of Dreyfusism and best described its philosophical originality. Péguy wrote at the time, "Betterment through suffering is a Christian supposition, and I am not a Christian. I have seen around me many kinds of suffering that were not literal or figurative: they harmed men the way glanders harms a horse. I myself favor betterment through the persistence of good health" (*Cahiers de la quinzaine*, 5 February 1900).

16. Raymond Abellio, *Les Militants* (Paris: Gallimard, 1975), 142–43.

17. Pivertists—named after their leader, Maurice Pivert—constituted the pacifist wing of the sfio (see below). —Intro.

18. Robert Dérathé, *Jean-Jacques Rousseau et la Science politique de son temps* (Paris: Vrin, 1970), 270. Dérathé adds: "Neither the two houses of the British government nor the Estates General of the Netherlands had the character of our parliamentary assemblies. So we should not expect Rousseau to judge the parliamentary regime in the same way that a man of the twentieth century could."

19. Pierre Rosanvallon, *Le Capitalisme utopique* (Paris: Editions du Seuil, 1979).

20. Pierre Monatte, *La Révolution prolétarienne*, 25 May 1935; quoted in Jean-Pierre Rioux, *Révolutionnaires du Front Populaire* (Paris: Union générale d'éditions, 1973).

21. The trade-union group Lutte de classes [class struggle], January 1937, in Rioux, *Révolutionnaires*, 290.

22. "La victoire en chantant" (victory while singing) are words taken

from "Chant de départ," the song sung by French soldiers as they marched off to fight in World War I. Even after the war, the song was taught to schoolchildren and sung as an expression of French patriotism. —Translator

23. "Bilan, perspectives, tâches," *Socialisme ou Barbarie*, March–May 1957, 1.

24. Pierre Rolle, "Socialisme ou Barbarie," *Non!* 8 (July–August 1981): 136.

25. See *Socialisme ou Barbarie*, March–April 1949, 44.

26. *Socialisme ou Barbarie*, March–May 1957, 16–17 (emphasis added).

27. Mario Tronti, *Ouvriers et Capital* (Editions Christian Bourgois, 1977).

28. *Notre royaume est une prison*, supplement to *La Guerre sociale* 3 (October 1980).

29. *De l'exploitation dans les camps à l'exploitation des camps*, supplement to *La Guerre sociale* 3 (May 1981): 13.

30. *Socialisme ou Barbarie* 12, August–September 1953.

31. Pierre Guillaume, quoted in Thion, ed., *Vérité historique*, 139.

32. La Vieille Taupe closed its doors as a bookstore in 1972; it was transformed into a publishing house in 1978 in an effort to help spread the news about the nonexistence of the gas chambers. Certain founders of La Vieille Taupe did not have any affinity for Guillaume's new crusade, and they let that fact be known loudly and clearly. Such was the case for Jacques Baynac, in particular. This goes to show that there is always a margin of uncertainty left open to what in old-fashioned terms is called morality and that even the most rigid ideology is not capable of extinguishing common sense in everyone.

33. See Fresco, "Les Redresseurs de morts." [The French term *re-dresseurs de morts*, translated here as "those who put the dead back on their feet," is a play on the words in the expression *redresseurs de torts*, righters of wrongs. —Trans.]

34. Amedeo Bordiga, "Le marxisme des bègues," *Russie et Révolution dans la théorie marxiste* (Paris: Editions Spartacus, 1978), 135, 154.

35. Jaurès, "Le manifeste communiste," 21.

36. Charles Péguy, "L'affaire Dreyfus et la crise du parti socialiste," *Revue blanche*, September 1899, 135.

37. Franz L. Neumann, *Behemoth: The Structure and Practice of Na-*

tional Socialism; quoted in Pierre Ayçoberry, *The Nazi Question: An Essay on the Interpretations of National Socialism (1922–75)*, trans. Robert Hurley (New York: Random House, 1981), 94.

38. *Notre royaume est une prison*.

2. WAR LOGIC AND *LANGUE DE BOIS*

1. Testimony of Roger Garaudy, in *Le Procès Kravchenko*, a review of the proceedings (Paris: Albin Michel, 1949). [For Garaudy's role in the most recent flare-up of the Holocaust denial in France, see the introduction to the present work. —Intro.]

2. Testimony of Dr. Aboulker, in *Le Procès Kravchenko*.

3. Master Pathelin, hero of the mid–fifteenth-century comedy *La Farce du Maître Pathelin*, is a wily lawyer adept at getting what he wants through trickery and ruse. —Intro.

4. Pierre Daix, *J'ai cru au matin* (Paris: Laffont, 1976), 232.

5. *Langue de bois* ("wooden tongue") is the name that those in France who opposed the Soviet regime gave to the hollow official discourse of Communist Party leaders. Today the term is applied to all political discourse laced with stock phrases and ideological clichés. —Trans.

6. From *Pravda*, quoted in *Franc-Tireur*, 2 February 1949.

7. Jean Baudrillard, *La Société de consommation* (Paris: Gallimard, 1971), 187–88.

8. Guy Debord, *The Society of the Spectacle* (Detroit: Red & Black, 1983), par. 24.

9. Jean Lacouture, *Survive le peuple cambodgien!* (Paris: Editions du Seuil, 1978), 90.

10. For a detailed recent history of the Pol Pot regime and the Cambodian genocide, see Ben Kiernan, *The Pol Pot Regime: Race, Power, and Genocide under the Khmer Rouge* (New Haven: Yale University Press, 1966). —Intro.

11. Lacouture, *Survive le peuple cambodgien!*, 5.

12. Régis Debray, in *La Machine à conter*, *Change* 38 (October 1979): 110 (emphasis added).

13. Noam Chomsky, in *La Machine à conter*, *Change* 38 (October 1979): 106.

14. The two hundred families to which Finkielkraut refers are the mythical wealthy families who supposedly controlled all wealth and power in Third Republic France. They are frequently denounced in right-wing and anti-Semitic literature and propaganda of the time. —Intro.

15. By writing the preface for Faurisson's book, Chomsky came to the aid of a *colleague*. One would like to believe that the champion of protest against the war in Vietnam got carried away in his liberalism and that through Faurisson he is defending the right to the free expression of ideas he himself considers to be most shocking. But such is not the case. Chomsky's solidarity goes well beyond such legal or formal support. He uses the same devices to deny the Cambodian genocide that Faurisson uses to deny the extermination of Jews. And if he takes a particular interest in the attempts to normalize Nazism, it is because he finds it intolerable that anyone should rival Uncle Sam for the title of absolute enemy. Hitler, the villain that a West short on innocence loves to hate? How could Chomsky fail to appreciate this argument when he attributes the same sacrificial function to Pol Pot? He hates imperialism, but he hates history even more for having *jumped the track*, for having engendered horrors that cannot be directly imputed to the Western world enlisted under the Yankee banner. Prophets do not like it when the real exceeds all prophecy. Through the negation, Chomsky is getting even with the facts; he is punishing reality for its disobedience and making it pay for its insolence. He thus quite naturally and logically takes up a position beside those who resent the past, with a passion known only to those who feel they have been swindled by history. Such is Chomsky or *Americano-centrism* taken to the extreme.

16. It was in order to respond to the success of *Roots* on a competing channel that one of the major American television networks decided to produce *Holocaust*, an undertaking requiring a family, a minority, and tears. The principle of equivalence was inscribed in the project from its very inception. And what was its most tangible result? The replacement of the word "genocide" with the word "holocaust" in everyday vocabulary. The massacre of a people became its immolation to God; a primary metaphysics took possession of an event that should have si-

lenced any and all words of justification; irremediable horror
was surreptitiously cloaked in sacrificial significance. Just what,
in fact, is a holocaust? "A religious sacrifice in which the victim
is totally consumed by fire," according to the dictionary. And the
Bible specifically indicates, "This combustion has an odor that
is pleasing to the Lord." One could argue that the theological
meaning has disappeared and only the idea of consummation
subsists today. Maybe so. The fact remains that we now use a
misleading term to refer to the genocide. We can only hope that
the word's original meaning has been forgotten and that it does
not *completely* distort the reality it now denotes.

17. For a discussion of the controversy surrounding the screening
of the American miniseries *Holocaust* on French television in
February–March 1979, see Henry Rousso, *The Vichy Syndrome:
History and Memory in France since 1944* (Cambridge: Harvard
University Press, 1991), 144–47. —Intro.

18. In Chomsky's words, "what the totalitarian State does by force,
democracy has to do by propaganda" (*La Machine à conter*, 118).

19. Gustave Flaubert, quoted in Jean-Paul Sartre, *The Family Idiot*,
trans. Carol Cosman, 5 vols. (Chicago: University of Chicago
Press, 1981–93), 1:606.

3. THE DISILLUSIONED GENERATION

1. Thion, ed., *Vérité historique*, 166.

2. A *pleureur* is someone who is easily or often moved to tears. The
term also signifies a person hired to cry at a funeral. —Trans.

3. Maurice Blanchot, *The Writing of the Disaster*, trans. Ann Smock
(Lincoln: University of Nebraska Press, 1986), 82.

4. Dominique Frot, *Libération*, 9 July 1981 (emphasis added).

5. "And you, Finkielkraut? Are you faceless? Are you speaking from
out of the blue? Just where do you imagine yourself situated, to
speak so disparagingly of a generation that is, after all, your very
own?"

   "I do not know *from whence* I speak. What I do know is that
'submitting to a generational mentality' (Kundera) is not an in-
evitability; it is a conformity, the most modern conformity there

is. What's the use in thinking if one's thinking merely follows the generational trend?"

6. The matter we are considering is problematic for the classic confrontation of extremists and liberals since it points out the existence of a hybrid figure, liberal fanaticism.

7. Margarete Buber-Neumann, *Déportée en Sibérie* (Paris: Editions du Seuil, 1949), 20.

8. Elie Wiesel, *Night*, trans. Stella Rodway (New York: Bantam Books, 1982), 4.

9. Walter Laquer, *The Terrible Secret, an Investigation into the Suppression of Information about Hitler's "Final Solution"* (London: Weidenfeld & Nicolson, 1980), 125.

10. Hermann Broch, *Les Somnambules* (Paris: Gallimard, 1957), 130.

11. Georges Wellers, of the Centre de Documentation Juive in Paris, was, according to Florent Brayard, "undoubtedly the first person to respond scientifically to the mystifications of the revisionists." Following the publication of Faurisson's revisionist claims in *Le Monde* in December 1978, Wellers responded in the same newspaper in an article entitled "An Abundance of Evidence." See Brayard, *Comment l'idée vint à M. Rassinier*, 352–57. —Intro.

12. Georges Wellers, *Les chambres à gaz ont existé* (Paris: Gallimard, 1980), 82.

13. As for the so-called evidence in the Nuremberg trial, it is suspect because it was upheld by a court. The nonbelievers' reasoning can be reconstituted as follows: the Moscow trials were rigged; there was a trial in Nuremberg; therefore, the Nuremberg trial was rigged.

14. Leftist radical and brother of the leader of the May 1968 student revolts, "Dany the Red," Jean-Gabriel ("Gaby") Cohn-Bendit defended Faurisson on the grounds that "freedom of speech . . . must be total and not subject to the least restriction." In a letter read before the court during Faurisson's trial, Cohn-Bendit also denied the existence of the gas chambers and denounced those who insisted that such chambers in fact existed. Like Faurisson (and more recently Roger Garaudy), Cohn-Bendit also denounced those who he claimed exploited the victims of the Holocaust to justify the politics of the State of Israel. Cohn-

Bendit's letter, entitled "A Question of Principle," is reproduced in Thion, ed., *Vérité historique*, 131–33. —Intro.

15. Jean-Gabriel Cohn-Bendit, "Génocide, chambres à gaz, des procès au débat," *L'Anti-Mythes* 25.

16. Jean-Paul Sartre, *Critique de la raison dialectique* (Paris: Gallimard, 1960), 34.

17. This expression, which means "everyone is beautiful, everyone is nice," is the title of a popular French film of the early 1970s. —Trans.

18. Pierre Vidal-Naquet, "Un Eichmann de papier," *Esprit*, September 1980; reprinted in Vidal-Naquet, *Les Juifs, la Mémoire et le Présent*, vol. 1 (Paris: F. Maspero, 1981). This footnote recognizes only one of a wealth of observations I owe to Vidal-Naquet's work.

19. Aleksandr I. Solzhenitsyn, *The Gulag Archipelago, 1918–1956: An Experiment in Literary Investigation*, trans. Thomas P. Whitney, pts. 1–4 (New York: Harper & Row, 1975), 331.

20. Solzhenitsyn, *The Gulag Archipelago*, 336.

21. The title of a novel by Louis-Ferdinand Céline, *Le casse-pipe* can be translated "the front." The popular expression *casser sa pipe* (literally, "to break one's pipe") means "to die." The phrase *le casse-pipe* designates both a shooting gallery at fairs where targets are clay pipes and, by extension, the front line of a combat zone, where the risk of death is great. —Trans.

22. Philosopher, writer, and occasional left-wing activist during the interwar years, Emmanuel Berl came from a wealthy Parisian Jewish family and was related to Marcel Proust and Henri Bergson. During the 1930s, he was friends with writers, artists, and intellectuals of all political stripes and was the editor of the prestigious leftist review *Marianne*. A decorated veteran of the First World War (hence his pacifism), Berl was briefly persuaded to write speeches for Philippe Pétain during the Occupation and then retired from politics. He died in 1976. —Intro.

23. Paul Rassinier, *Le Véritable Procès Eichmann ou les Vainqueurs incorrigibles* (Paris: Editions Les Sept Couleurs, 1962), 10.

24. David Rousset, *L'Univers concentrationnaire* (Paris: Editions de Minuit, 1965), 182.

25. Paul Rassinier, *Le Mensonge d'Ulysse* (Paris: La Vieille Taupe, 1979), 28.

26. Rassinier, *Le Mensonge d'Ulysse*, 28.

27. *Le Mensonge d'Ulysse*, 170.

28. We are told repeatedly and with increasing insistence that the twentieth century is the *century of war*. And that Céline is its bard. Céline, the poet of the apocalypse; Céline, "the historian of the century, a century that is not simply made up of dates, governments and coups d'état, of changes of regime or class struggles but simply, and sinisterly, of wars and charnel house productions—that is to say, of a prehistoric treatment of the multiple" (Philippe Muray, *Céline* [Paris: Editions du Seuil, 1981], 50); Céline, who uncovered the incurable horror of the world in his novels and who sought to cure the world in his pamphlets. But, to the contrary, is it the specificity of the twentieth century to have shattered the concept of war? The two great world conflicts cannot be reduced to the same terms, and Céline the novelist makes a very poor prophet to the extent that he seeks to subsume the era in a single image: "carnassial hysteria."

29. On the night of 6 February 1934, members of extreme right-wing and antidemocratic leagues including Action Française, Solidarité Française, and the Jeunesse Patriotes rioted at the Place de la Concorde and attempted to overthrow the government by storming the Chamber of Deputies across the Seine. The riots were prompted in large part by revelations of government corruption in the context of the Stavisky affair. The near-collapse of democracy in France on 6 February galvanized the left and led eventually to the Popular Front electoral victory in spring 1936.

    sfio (Section Française de l'Internationale Ouvrière) was the acronym commonly used to designate the French Socialist Party from its unification in 1905 through the interwar years. —Intro.

30. Paul Rassinier, *Candasse ou le Huitième Péché capital* (Paris: Amitié par le Livre, 1955), 283. As indicated by its title, this autobiographical account resembles Voltaire's *Candide* in the way it is written—hence its style and bizarre place-names.

31. Paul Rassinier, *Les Responsables de la Seconde Guerre mondiale* (Nouvelles Editions latines, 1967), 106.

32. Paul Rassinier, *Ulysse trahi par les siens* (Paris: La Vieille Taupe, 1980), 19.

4. IN SEARCH OF THE TRUE VICTIMS

1. Thion, ed., *Vérité historique*, 165.
2. Edward Saïd, "Les origines intellectuelles de l'impérialisme et du sionisme," in *Sionisme et Racisme: une question qui demande réponse* (Paris: Editions Le Sycomore, 1979), 164.
3. Saïd, "Les origines intellectuelles," 168.
4. Abdullah Sharafuddin (opening address at the International Symposium on Zionism and Racism, Tripoli, Lebanon, July 1976), 16.
5. On 1 September 1981—following the meeting of Claude Cheysson with Yasser Arafat—Raymonda Tawil, in Jerusalem, hailed "the courageous attitude of a former Resistance member who fought against Nazism. Through his words, he has recognized the right of all peoples, including the Palestinian people, to fight against occupation." Can you imagine Jean Moulin calling the press together on a September day in 1942 in order to exhort his countrymen to fight against the invader and to congratulate himself for the diplomatic progress made by General de Gaulle in London? I say this not to justify the disquieting politics of Israel but to restore the distance that a purely incantatory language is designed to abolish.
6. Anis el Qasem, "Racisme et paix mondiale," in *Sionisme et Racisme: une question qui demande réponse* (Paris: Editions Le Sycomore, 1979), 29.
7. Tahar Ben Jelloun, "Seul face au monde," *Le Monde*, 24 July 1981, 2 (emphasis added).
8. Another example—an even more gripping one, if that is possible—goes as follows: "Why couldn't we be Salvadorans or Afghans, or better yet, white men from the West? Then the world would not be indifferent to our deaths. Chiefs of state, organizations of all sorts, the pope, and public opinion would all rise up to proclaim their indignation at our massacre. They would be incapable of finding words harsh enough to condemn this state-sponsored terrorism that strikes at the heart of the people of a

UN member-state. Alas *we are merely Lebanese and Palestinians*, and our aggressors are Jewish. We are but a small fraction of the Third World. And the people killing us think they have free rein *because they say they are the chosen people*. And the West, which remained silent when it was not acting as Hitler's accomplice at the time of the Jewish genocide, is silent again today because it is Jews who are killing Arabs." Who is this flamboyant Fedayin, this pathetic peasant, this Eastern refugee crazed with rage? His name is Georges Montaron, he runs the weekly *Témoignage chrétien*, and he lives in Paris-sur-Seine. Exemplary in its Third World eloquence, this bit of feverish rhetoric combines the spectator and the maquisard in one and the same revolt. We are all Palestinians bombed by the chosen people. Two discourses make this vengeful, lying "we" possible: the Marxist transposition of Christianity, which sees the modern incarnation of the Savior in the world's most disadvantaged; and Christianity pure and simple, or at least the version of it that continues to reproach the Jews for the arrogance of being the chosen people and for the murder of the God-made-man. When the diffuse Christianity of revolutionary thought is combined with explicitly Christian engagement, the Jews are doubly guilty: of persecuting the Palestinians and of crucifying the Messiah a second time. Two dramas are being played out together: the Resistance, with the Jew in the role of the Nazi; and the crucifixion, with the Jew in the role of the Jew. (The text cited—with my emphasis added—appeared in *Témoignage chrétien*, 27 July 1981.)

9. Raphaël Lemkin, *Axis Rule in Occupied Europe: Laws of Occupation, Analysis of Government, Proposals for Redress* (Washington DC: Carnegie Endowment for International Peace, Division of International Law, 1944). [Here I have simply translated the French version back into English. —Trans.]

10. Occitanians are the inhabitants of the southern provinces of France collectively known as the Occitan or the *pays d'oc*. Their numerous dialects have been kept alive through the persistence of a literary tradition that revitalized itself at the end of the last century. Since the 1960s much of the region's literary production has become a literature of contestation, protesting a modern

world that has turned the rural Occitan into an alienated, underdeveloped area. —Trans.

11. Now, in fact, people are beginning to speak of a holocaust with reference to the scandal of world hunger. This is undoubtedly an attempt to awaken sleeping consciences by connecting the hallowed image of absolute Evil to the horrors of underdevelopment. For public indifference can no longer be attributed to *ignorance* as it once could. Thwarting the optimism of the Enlightenment (knowledge as moral progress), public indifference is now the result of *habit*. The more suffering that people see on their TV screens, the less concerned they feel. Current events demobilize them; images kill the feeling of obligation within them. The public is blasé: news reports fail to take their audience beyond the realm of everyday experience, and they insinuate the most monstrous realities into the everyday by marking them with the stamp of the déjà-vu.

In order to *break public opinion of this habit*, one is almost naturally led to up the ante. Famine attains the status of genocide, and the West's *responsibility* for the Third World's delayed development becomes the West's *extermination* of Third World peoples.

But confusion is not an effective remedy. In the attempt to identify two irreducible phenomena this way, they both become dematerialized. Moral conscience makes no progress, but unreality does. The Jewish genocide and the famine in poor countries are absorbed in a sort of black hole, in a concept whose overuse condemns it to *insignificance*: the Holocaust.

12. Christian Colombani, "Members of the University Community Clash over the Faurisson Case," *Le Monde*, 30 June 1981.

13. Along with Cohn-Bendit, Assous and Rittersporn collaborated with Serge Thion in assembling documents included in *Vérité historique ou vérité politique?*. During the media debate surrounding Faurisson's claims, Assous also signed a petition in defense of Rassinier and in favor of a serious "historical" investigation of his theses. See Thion, ed., *Vérité historique*, 128–30. —Intro.

14. Guy Hocquenghem, preface to *Les Hommes au triangle rose*, by Heinz Heger (Persona, 1981), 9.

15. Hocquenghem, preface to *Les Hommes*, 10.

16. Faurisson, *Mémoire en défense*, 3.
17. See Hocquenghem, preface to *Les Hommes*, 21.
18. The NKVD (Soviet People's Commissariat for Internal Affairs) was the predecessor of the KGB. —Intro.
19. Jean Plumyène, "Les nations romantiques," *Histoire du nationalisme. Le XIXe siècle* (Paris: Fayard), 148.
20. Fyodor Dostoevsky, quoted in David J. Goldstein, *Dostoïevski et les Juifs* (Paris: Gallimard, 1976), 126.
21. Hocquenghem, preface to *Les Hommes*, 8.
22. "Newspeak" is the name George Orwell gives to the official language of Oceania, the fictional country in which he sets *1984*. We live in a free country; Power does not concern itself with the existence of words; and yet just as in *1984*, the reality of history and the survival of the past depend on the way we use language.

EPILOGUE: PREJUDICE AND PARADOX

1. Emmanuel Lévinas, "Simone Veil against the Bible," *Difficult Freedom: Essays on Judaism*, trans. Seán Hand (Baltimore: Johns Hopkins University Press, 1990), 141.
2. In Bergsonian terms, it will be said that the rejection of the State of Israel feels solid, justified enough, natural enough to carry out automatically and over time a retrograde movement. In Begin's mirror the genocide is either a banal massacre or even a well-deserved punishment. The image of Tsahal, the Israeli army, is reflected behind it in an indefinite past: it is the tragic effect of the *logic of retrospection* that "cannot not throw current realities back into the past, to the state of possibilities or of virtualities, so that what is brought about today must have always been so, in his view." See Henri Bergson, *La Pensée et le Mouvant* (Paris: Presse Universitaire de la France, 1975), 19.

Index

antifascism, 14–15; proletariat
  view of, 24
anti-Semitism: compared with
  antifascism, 33; disappearance
  of, 121; as diversion from
  capitalistic misdeeds, 24–25;
  future of, 117; political value of,
  32; of rivalry, 112; viewed by
  Socialists, 9
Arendt, Hannah, 87
Assassins of Memory (Vidal-
  Naquet), xxiv–xxv

barbarity, 98–100; and definition
  of Capital and Revolution, 21;
  of exploitation, 62; nonfascist,
  119; politics of, 58; Socialism
  or, 21–22
Bardèche, Maurice, xviii
Brayard, Florent, xxii

Cambodia, 46–49
capitalism, the working class
  defending, 24
Le casse-pipe (Céline), 80–81
Castro, Fidel, 60
Céline, Louis-Ferdinand, 80–81,
  138 n.28
Chomsky, Noam, xxi, xxv–xxvi, 1,
  48–49, 134 n.15

Colombani, Christian, 103–4
conspirationalist judeophobia,
  xviii, 127 n.16

Debray, Régis, 48–49
Le Drame des Juifs européens
  (Rassinier), xx
Dreyfus affair, xxix, 6–10, 25, 106

L'Evénement du jeudi, xi, xxx

falsification of words, 114–15
Father Pierre (Henry Grouès), xi,
  xiv–xviii
Faurisson, Robert, xx–xxviii, 1–4,
  27–28, 56; against dissemination
  of information, 52; against
  dogmatism, 57; explaining
  revisionism, 77; perceived
  as The Jew, 106; trial of,
  xxvi–xxviii, 63–64
Finkielkraut, Alain, xxviii–xxx

Garaudy, Roger, xii–xix; on
  Kravchenko, 38
Gayssot Law, xiii, 126 n.6
genocide, 95; as justification
  for Israel, 91; and legitimacy,
  117; as mark of respectability,
  114; origin of word, 97–98;

Index

Index

In the *Texts and Contexts* series

*Antisemitism, Misogyny, and
the Logic of Cultural
Difference: Cesare Lombroso
and Matilde Serao*
By Nancy A. Harrowitz

Opera: Desire, Disease, Death
By Linda Hutcheon
and Michael Hutcheon

Poetic Process
By W. G. Kudszus

*Keepers of the Motherland:
German Texts by Jewish
Women Writers*
By Dagmar C. G. Lorenz

*Madness and Art: The Life
and Works of Adolf Wölfli*
By Walter Morgenthaler
Translated and with an
introduction by Aaron
H. Esman in collaboration
with Elka Spoerri

*Organic Memory:
History and the Body in the
Late Nineteenth and Early
Twentieth Centuries*
By Laura Otis

*Crack Wars: Literature,
Addiction, Mania*
By Avital Ronell

*Finitude's Score: Essays for
the End of the Millennium*
By Avital Ronell